MEN'S COMEDIC MONOLOGUES THAT ARE ACTUALLY FUNNY

MEN'S COMEDIC MONOLOGUES THAT ARE ACTUALLY FUNNY

Edited by

ALISHA GADDIS

APPLAUSE
THEATRE & CINEMA BOOKS
An Imprint of Hal Leonard Corporation

Published in 2015 by Applause Theatre & Cinema Books
An Imprint of Hal Leonard Corporation
7777 West Bluemound Road
Milwaukee, WI 53213

Trade Book Division Editorial Offices
33 Plymouth St., Montclair, NJ 07042

Printed in the United States of America

Book design by UB Communications

Library of Congress Cataloging-in-Publication Data is available upon request.

ISBN 978-1-4803-9681-4

www.applausebooks.com

Contents

Contents vii

Introduction

I know how it goes—because we have been there.

You have an audition. One where you are supposed to be funny. Really funny. They want you to actually make them laugh...in an audition. And you want to be funny, so funny you book the job, land the part, steal the show!

But you have to have a comedic monologue, and everything you read is lame semiweird, and from 1983.

And you don't want that. You don't want to look like an idiot with a bad monologue or a Flock of Seagulls haircut. Leave the past in the past and prepare for hip, fresh, and hilariously now.

This book was conceived because I know a lot of funny people. People that make a living off of being funny. Let these funny people help you make a living off being funny yourself.

Now's the time to share the love and hilarity.

Pick a monologue. Book that job. Steal the show. Make them laugh.

And for goodness' sake, don't do a monologue that isn't *actually* funny ever again.

Alisha Gaddis

Into the Woods with Love

Alisha Gaddis

PAUL, 25–45

PAUL *is a park ranger, who is obsessed with the job. He is drunk with love for his woods. Here, he is acting as a tour guide.*

PAUL   Watch your head here comes the branch of *Ulmus castaneifolia* or chestnut-leafed elm for those of you who are not in. the. know.

Watch your head. Watch your head. Right this way.

My name is Paul, as my nametag reads, no, not Paul Bunyon—although some say I am built like an ox. [*Chuckles to himself.*]

Joking.

[*Clears throat.*] I am THE Park Ranger here at Kumquatanation National Park and Recreation Center. I started my training as an intern when I was a young twelve-year-old lad, and have worked my way up the competitive park ranger ladder ever since. It was as vicious and backstabbing as I am sure you all are thinking—but worth the risks. You don't get this hat by just looking pretty. No siree.

Now, it is my duty to show you the grounds. Something I take seriously, because it is serious.

Some might say I OWN these woods. I say that. I say that a lot, actually.

This is my woods. My forest. My national land. I love my wood.

It may not bear my name, but we know each other. We get each other, intimately. By law it is yours, the people's, as well as mine. Not something I agree with, but my petitions have been denied several times.

[*Looks off wistfully—sees boy by poisonous bush.*]

Hey—boy!—get away from that pretty berry bush!—It may look ripe and delicious like a woman's loin, but it will eat you alive and leave you burning. Trust me. I've been there.

Okay. Where was I?

Let me point out that over to the left is the Gazebo of Dreams under the *Salix babylonica*—or weeping willow—as you all call it. Such a sad name. For a glorious creature. Some people love the gazebo—I love the tree. Look at her. Sheer beauty, grace, simple elegance. Just needs to be hugged. Tree hugged.

Alright. As your park ranger and a park ranger to all—I must point out this creek. Look at all those families picnicking near. I wouldn't do that if I were you. This creek has excess fecal matter.

[*Beat.*]

No. Not human. Don't be ridiculous. Animal fecal matter. For some reason animals love to shit in this creek. They shit up Shit Creek and there is nothing we can do to stop it. Let nature be nature. And don't get too close while posing for your photos.

Shit Creek is not a metaphor. It is real. It is natural. It is life.

Over to your right you can see the Bridge of New Beginnings arching over Shit Creek. Some may call that ironic. I call it that. I call it that a lot.

Everyone seems to think this is a great place for pictures. If you choose to have your wedding here—you probably will, too.

I think it is a great place to watch the frolicking young *cervidaes*, or like the common idiot calls them—deer. I call them friends. I call them that a lot.

So, this concludes the tour. I wish you all the best as future husband and wife, mating is natural after all. And remember if you have your special day here at Kumquatanation National Park and Recreation Center, please tell your guests to only leave footprints and take away memories.

But be careful—these woods will take your heart and whisper your name. Sweet nothings, sweet nothings.

Also, the porta-potties are over the hill on the right. 'Cause this land was made for you and me. But mostly me.

Thanksgiving Blessings

Carla Cackowski

GOODMAN CLANCY, 30s to 60s

GOODMAN CLANCY, *a Pilgrim, speaks privately to his wife in front of a wigwam.*

GOODMAN CLANCY   Now here this, Goody Clancy. If I fail to negotiate food plentiful enough for our family and community, all of us are fated to starve to death. Make no mistake, wife, I vow to secure a delicious feast from the natives.

[*The natives approach.*]

Good morrow, Chief Tomahay. Ah, yes, this is mine wife, Goody Clancy. And yours? Squaw? For serious? Squaw. Interesting name. Very…native-y. The pleasure is ours.

[GOODMAN CLANCY *steps forward to welcome Squaw. She cowers from him.*]

Forgive me. I didn't mean to scare ye, Squaw. Ye have never seen my kind up close.

[GOODMAN CLANCY *elbows the Chief.*]

Only but briefly while raping and pillaging your tribe, ay?

[GOODMAN CLANCY *reacts to his wife hitting his arm.*]

A joke! [*Clears throat.*] Apologies. That was inappropriate. I'm nervous. Moving on! I have called ye here, Chief Tomahay, because mine community is scared. Bellies empty. Nutrition denied. Festive dinner parties cancelled—Chief Tomahay, we are starving to death! I have seen your majestic crops. Might we negotiate a trade? Yes, yes, we get it. Thou can provide for yourself. No need to rub it in. But is there nothing ye can think of that we could trade?

Shoes? Shoes. Really? Okey dokey. Shoes. Ye are in luck! For mine wife's feet are adorned with a sole of special leather from the other side of the world. Well, England, of course. What did thou expect me to say? France? Yuck!

Come on, Goody Clancy. Give me your shoes. Yes, yes, I know, ye need shoes, but I need my shoes even more. I am the man, for goodness sake…I have hunting and gathering to do in these shoes!

[GOODMAN CLANCY *hands Goody's shoes to the Chief and is given a sack of potatoes in return.*]

Oh, heavenly day! Potatoes! Many blessings on your tribe, Chief Tomahay! Unfortunately, potatoes do not a feast make. Chief, perhaps there is something else your tribe desires? Well, what sort of white man would I be if I did not push my luck?

Shoes? Again? More shoes. Really? [*Whispers to wife.*] Wife, does thou have any more shoes? [*Rolls eyes.*] Oh, fine. Here. Take mine.

[GOODMAN CLANCY *takes off his own shoes and hands them to the Chief. He is given another sack in return.*]

Corn. Yum yum. Indeed. Many blessings, Chief.

Mayhaps ye have some protein? Any meat? Oh, good! What would ye like to trade? Please don't say it…really? Shoes? Again? But you've got such nice moccasins adorning your feet. Our shoes are zero in ways of fashion. Look at the tassels thou has on those things!

Okay, okay. Fine. Ye want shoes…Chief Tomahay, I am seriously in lack of shoes of the human variety at the moment, but my horse—what do ye say about horse shoes? Yes? Yes!

[*The Chief hands* GOODMAN CLANCY *a bird for trade.*]

A turkey! I prefer chicken, but traders can't be choosers.

Well done, everyone! Look what good can come of this life when one sets aside their values and works toward a common goal of feeding mine community's mouth-holes.

Chief Tomahay, ye have been very kind. So kind, in fact, ye should join us for a feast to celebrate our good fortunes.

Thou would rather stab thouself with a spear than break bread with a white man? Wow. That's a lot of judgment, Chief. Come now, Goody Clancy. We have finished our business with the natives.

[GOODMAN CLANCY *grabs his wife's arm to usher her away.*]

Thou cannot even begin to understand how hard our lives have been. Do not judge me until ye walk a day in mine shoes!

[*He turns to leave, then quickly turns back.*]

Pardon me. I did not realize how quickly mine toes would freeze in this weather. Might I borrow some moccasins for the walk home?

Get (Back) Together

Jeff Passino

ALEX, 20s to 40s

ALEX *is shopping, in the dairy aisle at a Pavilion's grocery store.*

ALEX   And here I thought the toughest decision I would make today would be to spend the extra dollar for organic milk or not, but then you want to know...what exactly? If we can get back together? And you are seriously not joking about this. You are not another dream or drunken hallucination. And you ARE doing this here in Pavilion's. Okay.

Obviously, I have had a lot of time to think about this over the past...year. Has it really been a year? I guess a couple weeks shy of a year, technically, but it's felt like a fucking eternity, so let's just go ahead and round up to a year, shall we?

Yes. The answer is yes. I want to get back to what we had. I want to not feel this loneliness or carry around this heavy sadness anymore. I want someone to laugh with about all the stupid shit we say and do. I want to take someone out to eat, to the movies. I want to share the things I love and see them for the first time through new eyes. I want to come home at the end of the day and hear about someone's day that I actually care about, 'cause Heidi, at work, if I hear one more story about her sister, so help me. But mostly I miss having someone there in bed with me at night. I miss running my fingers down your back and kissing you before I go to sleep. And then, in the morning, waking to see you still sleeping and then annoying the shit out of you 'cause we've slept too long and have to get going immediately.

So yes, I absolutely want to get back to all of that. I miss all of that so much, every day. And I have had so much time to realize a lot of the mistakes I made. I relied too heavily on letting my actions speak for themselves about how much I love you. I didn't take the chance every day to tell you how beautiful I found you. It's not because you needed it said or like the whole world was ignorant to the fact that you are a knockout, but because you deserve to hear that, every day, and I shouldn't have kept it to myself. I obviously had my faults. I've still got most of them. Quite frankly, I'm still not sure how exactly I am supposed to stop farting in bed. Who goes eight hours WITHOUT farting? It is probably impossible and, if not, then I'm sure unhealthy to do so. That aside, I loved you too quietly. Which I understand the irony, as that was another big complaint about my farting. But I was scared to love you. I was scared you would leave me. And maybe in the end that became a self-fulfilling prophecy. Maybe that is why you left me? Maybe you left 'cause you were too scared of loving me? I don't really know the answers there, do I? The point is that was a stupid thing for me to do, because no matter how much I would try to act, outwardly, that I wasn't madly in love with you, it wouldn't keep that from being a reality inside me, and so ultimately all I was doing was not letting myself live my truth. And that was stupid of me.

So do I want to get back to that time and fix all those parts? Yes, I do. Do I want to get back to having a relationship with the types of moments we shared? Yes, I do. Absolutely. Do I want to get back together with you? No way.

No way, because despite my obvious flaws and despite you being ridiculously good-looking...seriously, you've done something new with your hair and, though I wouldn't have thought it possible before, it actually suits you better and is extremely sexy and making it very hard to stand my ground on all of this, but I've got to. Regardless, compliments to your hairdresser. Truly. Where was I? Oh yes...despite all of that, I was really pretty awesome to you. I took you to amazing places and gave you so many amazing first-time experiences. When you were sick I took you in, with no regard for my own health, and fed you a steady diet of soup, movies, and sleep till you were better. When you would ask me advice on major life decisions, I would give them but then push you to follow YOUR gut, even when that was the opposite of what I really wanted you to do. I wanted you to be and feel like the strong independent woman you are. When you were diagnosed as being allergic to EVERYTHING, I learned every piece of food you were allergic to and made sure there was always multiple things you could eat at my place AND I modified every recipe for every dinner I cooked so that there was no gluten, nuts, soy, dairy, citrus, or celery. So much so that it was as if, for a year, I was allergic and had to stay away from those things as well. By the way, I am sorry if standing here in the milk aisle for so long is causing you to break out in hives. I did a LOT for you. I did it because that is what my love told me to do for you. And in turn your love, what? Told you to stay away from me when I was sick? To get angry at me for not making certain decisions for you? To lie to me? To take advantage of me? To cheat on me? To just one day leave me, and ignore me, pretending that everything we've done and gone through never happened for a whole year. I'm sorry, a couple weeks shy of a year. Well I deserve better than someone who treats me like that. That is my truth.

Now if you will excuse me, my cocoa crisps deserve this organic milk.

Moving In

Alessandra Rizzotti

PATRICK, 20-something

PATRICK *is a hot pool-boy type who is earnest, eager, and wanting to please everyone. He is at his best friend Shawn's home and has just been caught coming out of Shawn's father's bedroom. He is about to tell Shawn that he is in love with Shawn's father, and that he'll be moving in.*

PATRICK   I know you've been angry with me recently. And I value your friendship so much, so it's been hard holding this in and I really just want to tell you. Because you mean a lot to me. Shit. Ten years growing up together, going to college together, going up to Big Bear that one time…

Okay, here goes. Your dad and I are developing a really close relationship that actually happened up at the slopes when you were like, "Where did you go?" And I was like, "Nowhere." I know I'm your age and stuff so that might be weird for you, but I didn't grow up with a dad, as you know, so it's not that weird for me. I want you to know that my love for you as a brother, a friend, it was never because of my attraction to your dad. I totally sound like I have daddy issues… shit. I value you so much. I know my actions don't seem to say it now, but rather than being your friend, I want to be your second dad. I want to care for you like my own kid. Sounds fucked up, but that's actually how I felt about you before I became your friend.

So, I'll be around the house more often now. Doing chores and stuff, cleaning up after your brother. It might be a little weird at first seeing your best friend getting all parental, but I bet over time we'll be a happy family. Your dad wanted to tell you with me, but I just couldn't hold it in any longer because I'm so EXCITED. I'm really just pumped to be around even more often now. Aren't you?

Understandably, you're weirded out. Shit. I didn't mean to get selfish just now. This is probably like the time my mom came home from stripping and told me she was dating my stepbrother. I mean, except I'm outing your dad in front of you. Crap. That makes me a shithead. I hope you don't see it that way.

[PATRICK*'s partner walks in.*]

I was just telling John about us. He seems to be taking it fine. Why don't you sit down and I'll fix us some mimosas? Don't give me that look, Jerry. You know I can't hold surprises in.

[PATRICK *turns to his friend.*]

You're going to love living with me. And I know we usually call each other "bro," but maybe get used to calling me "dad" or "daddio" or "pops." "Pa"? "Bro pa"? Ha-ha, that's lame. "Dadster" is pretty good.

Sandwiches

Brandon Econ

WALTER MOORE, 39

WALTER MOORE *is the kind of guy that really tested the boundaries of his body, mind and spirit in college. When he got married he vowed to never go back to the "dark days". That doesn't mean he's ignorant however so when it comes to sniffing out the onset of bad behavior with his son his sense memory kicks in and he knows exactly what's going on. He doesn't want his son to miss out on experiences but he wants to make sure he understands the consequences. He's talking to his son at the top of the stairs in a two story townhouse.*

WALTER   Hey buddy, before you go to practice, I want to talk to you about something. Alright? So, I was in your room earlier today. I know what you're going to say—that's a violation of your privacy…and you're right. I'm sorry I did it. But I saw something while I was in there. I saw some crusts. Have you been eating sandwiches? Don't lie to me.

Pastrami on rye? Jesus, Brian. I thought your mother and I raised you better. You know pastrami on rye is a gateway sandwich, right? Listen to me. I'm not just your dad—I'm your friend.

It's just one sandwich? Yeah, now it is, but just you wait. Next it's going to be corned beef on rye, then it's the Rachel, and god forbid you start eating reubens. I know all about it alright. Your dad was a kid, too. Is it peer pressure? Your friends probably got you into this. Remember that boy, Tommy, up the street? Didn't he just get caught handing out PB&J's? Listen, son, I'm glad we caught this early on.

I'm not making a big deal out of it for nothing, alright? Let me tell you a story. Back when I was your age, maybe a little older, me and my buddies took a trip to New Orleans for spring break. We did it all, the French Quarter, the church of St. Expedite, the jazz clubs, the beach, everything. But that's also, unfortunately, where I discovered, muffulettas. I'm ashamed to say that in front of my own son, but your pops is addicted to muffulettas. Any chance I got, I'd try and get my hands on one. It got to the point that whenever I heard the pop of a lid, I'd go into a rage thinking it was someone opening a jar of giardiniera.

It's a kind of olive salad son. It's not important. The point is, I don't want that to be you. I don't want you to be walking down Bourbon Street with your friends and them having to physically pry you away from a deli window just because they're carving up mortadella.

Look—my hands are shaking.

Listen buddy, I know where you get it. Our whole family's this way. My father, your grandfather, used to place bologna on top of the toaster so it would drip onto the bread. I mean, I'm lucky. I've got your mother. If it wasn't for her, who knows where I'd be. I'd probably be giving out hand jobs just to lick a piece of provolone. But you're young—you've got your whole life ahead of you. Don't throw it away on a little meat and bread. Promise me.

That's a good boy. Alright, now you want to come downstairs and have a drink with your old man?

The Third Date

Deborah Gross

Premiered at the Hollywood Fringe Festival
in Los Angeles.

EVAN, 30s

EVAN *is on a third date. He has invited his date, Allie, to his apartment. They sit in silence on the couch, while Evan tries to think of another story to share to impress his date and show all his appealing characteristics.*

EVAN   What scares me? Nothing. I'm supercool. Okay. I'll be serious. Let me think.

I don't like to be scared. It's not my thing. So if, like, I'm scared of something, I conquer it.

So snakes, right? I was scared of snakes. I never had a bad experience with them or anything—I was just terrified of them. It was so bad that if I saw a snake on TV, I'd have to change the channel immediately. It was starting to not only affect my life but my loved ones as well, especially if they wanted to watch something on the Discovery Channel.

I'm being vulnerable. Don't laugh.

Like I was saying before, I can't stand being scared of things, so I finally had enough and called up a serpentarium and asked if I could come for a visit. By the way, did you know that snakes can swallow up to 85 percent more than their body weight.

It's true. I can tell you don't believe me. I'm going to look it up on my phone.

[*He takes out his phone.*]

I want you to know that it's the only reason why I'm taking it out. I'm going to "yahoo" it.

Okay.

Okay. "Yahooing" it. Usually girls like that joke. You know, because most people "google." Nevermind. Okay. It's like 20 percent. Whatever. Still kinda ridiculous.

[*Still looking at his phone.*]

No way. Oh, nothing. It's just my friend telling me something. Hold on. I don't want to be rude by ignoring him.

Sorry, what? No, I didn't go to a zoo. I went to a serpentarium.

I finally got up the balls to go and I had them put the snake on my shoulders.

No. Not like Britney Spears. I'm a fucking man.

I held the snake, all 220 pounds of him, like this... [*He stands and holds his hands up like Britney Spears.*] I stood there, sweating, crying, hyperventilating, for two hours till my body finally stopped shaking. It was super intense. So yeah, I conquered my fear. I still don't like snakes but at least I can watch them on TV now without changing the channel.

More wine?

To My Next Boss

Kenny Madrid

GEORGE, 26

GEORGE *was excited to enter the workforce after college, but quickly learned through various difficult and unfulfilling jobs, exactly why so many adults lose the spark of life. Some would call that spark happiness. The setting is in an office with no windows, not even frosted glass on the door. It is barren, cold, and a slightly blue tint to it as if David Fincher were directing. The fluorescent light flickers enough so that it's noticeable, but not enough to worry about fixing it. No art decorating the walls, it looks more like a room where people are fired than hired.*

GEORGE ~~I just wanted to~~ thank you for bringing me in to interview to be your assistant. I'm sure you've got a lot on your plate, but before I go I have a few questions. ~~It's common knowledge that~~ the interviewee should bring in a list of questions to appear as if we are truly interested in this job, but my experiences in the workplace have given me a greater insight into exactly the kind of questions I should be asking. I have written out a lengthy list so forgive me, but I hear bosses appreciate assistants being thorough.

Does your company match 401(k) contributions? Is my wage hourly, or will I be salaried? When does overtime kick in? After eight hours? Twelve hours? At all? Do you offer eye-care coverage in addition to the dental? ~~I love to bake, so do you~~

~~enjoy fresh-baked cooki~~es? Do you pretend to have any major diet restrictions because of the latest trends you hear about in Hollywood, i.e., gluten-free, paleo diet, veganism, pescatarianism, etcetera? Have you or has anyone else ever called you a "foodie?" Is your favorite restaurant all of the way across town, but somehow it will be my fault when there is traffic on the way there and back? Does the office keep healthy snacks readily available so that once I have completely given up on ever exercising again after spending fourteen-hour days in the office, I won't gain a ton of weight from ~~Skittles, Snickers, and~~ health bars that pretend to be good for you but in reality are just as awful as candy?

When I inevitably screw something up, as all humans do from time to time, will you act as if I just murdered your first AND second-born children no matter the size or frequency of the mistake? Speaking of families, do you have one? Will they ever see you? Or are you single but married to your work? Will you forget that I have a life outside of work? Should I just cut ties with friends and family right now? They don't matter, right? I'll just kid myself and say this isn't the way my career will always be? What kind of hobbies do you have that are really just veiled attempts at sounding like you have a life outside of work?

Are you big into mentoring? Most people in our industry don't want to be a career assistant; will you be interested in giving me tips on how you do your job so that one day I can use those tools myself? Will you take that interest from a paranoid standpoint, that I am trying to take your job from you despite your twenty years' experience in the industry? Will you say that you do wish to mentor and then somehow over the course of many months be too busy to ever sit down with me for five minutes, your own assistant, who has dedicated a significant portion of my life to your well-being?

Office decorating—off-limits, or completely frowned upon? I have a kooky sense of humor so forgive me if I put up some motivational posters, but ironically. Will you not approve of these posters but not want to say anything so I will just get the stink eye from you until I take them down of my own "free will?" What about office parties? Do people throw parties for birthdays in the office? Will I be able to attend these parties, or does one possible missed call take precedence over any fun I could take part in?

How loud can you scream? Should I bring earplugs? Or just leave all emotions at home? How soon before I will hope to hit every red light on the way to work just to keep me out of the office even if for only minutes more?

But I think most importantly, when do I start?

Bumpy Firsts

Mike McAleer

ROBBIE, 30

ROBBIE, 30, is an immature teenaged-boy stuck in an average man's body. He has gone from menial job to menial job since high school, and he currently works at a CVS. Here ROBBIE finally gets the courage to make a move on his elementary school crush, his first-grade teacher, Miss O'Donnell, as she shops for herpes medication.

ROBBIE   Miss O'Donnell? It's me! Robbie. Robbie Hamilton from your first-grade class back in 1988. Maybe if I take off my hat it will help you remember? But not for too long cuz the boss doesn't like us out of uniform. I know, right? I mean the nametag I understand, but the hat? What other pharmacy do you know that makes their employees wear a hat? Sorry, a red hat with white gemstone lettering. As if anybody could mistake me working here with this infectious disease diagram T-shirt they make us wear. No? That's okay, I guess I look pretty different now all grown up. No more braces, yay! Slightly no more hair, boo. Wow! It has been like twenty-six years since you've seen…we've seen each other. And you still don't look a day over angel on earth. Double wow! I cannot believe I just said that to you. Holy shit, you sure can take the kid out of Miss O'Donnell's Highland Park Elementary School first-grade class, but you can't take the Miss O'Donnell out of…Nevermind. Hey listen, do you remember when you had

all of us bring in gifts that Christmas to exchange with each
other? And all the girls were getting hairbrushes and My Little
Pony dolls, and the boys were getting mostly Micro Machines
and baseball cards. And everything was pretty awesome for
everybody, but if you remember, only one of your students
actually thought about you that Christmas, and he bought you
a small silver purse with gold buttons around the top. They
were fake gold, of course, and the whole thing didn't cost more
than a dollar from the dollar store, but you treated him like he
just gave you a Gucci bag or Prada or something. I was so
relieved because I was super embarrassed to bring you such a
cheap gift, but I really wanted to give you something nice, and
I was seven, so my choices were limited. Not anymore though.
I mean I get a super sweet discount here if there is anything
you want. Just let me know. I would totally do that for you,
Miss O'Donnell. You'll have to give me the cash, though, so
they don't see me use a credit card without my name on it. The
boss is really strict here. Anyway, the reason I brought up that
Christmas present story is because I feel like you gave me so
much back then, helping me grow into this awesome human
being I am today, and I think it's time I help you in return. So
that bump I see there above your lip . . . it looks just like the one
you had back when I gave you the Christmas present. You were
so happy, and you gave me the biggest hug, and you said, "I
want to give you the biggest kiss on the cheek right now, but I
can't because I have this little pimple here." Oh man, I'm
getting butterflies just thinking about it again. I really wanted
that kiss, Miss O'Donnell! I mean if the offer still stands . . . But
first, since I was seven at the time, and I didn't know any better,
I went on thinking for years that if you have a pimple on your
face, you cannot give other people kisses, not even on the
cheek. I mean this was okay to believe back in elementary

school when I didn't want to kiss any of the girls anyway, but when I hit high school, my face turned into the stuff dermatologists' nightmares are made of, and since I thought I wasn't allowed to kiss anybody for fear of what my crater face would do to them, I ended up alone for a very long time. "Get to the part where you want to help me," is what you're thinking, right? Right. Well, since I started working here at the end of last year, I learned to identify those types of bumps like the one above your lip today, like the one above your lip in '88. They aren't pimples! They're cold sores, often brought on by stress, and all you need to do is get some…Oh, I see you already have some Abreva in your cart…somebody must have already told you. Did that guy tell you about it? That old guy, the one you've been coming in here with every other Thursday afternoon, unless it's raining, in which case you two will come in on Friday instead and go to the back and grab two sixteen-ounce fizzy drinks before going to the pickup desk and grabbing your prescriptions and leaving? Did he also tell you that sometimes fortune cookies are wrong, and even though they might say that today is your lucky day and you should go for it, and I take that to mean that I'm finally going to talk to my beautiful first-grade teacher who I've seen in here but she hasn't seen me…nevermind. Okay, well it looks like you're all set here then. I'm going to get back to work before the boss comes out. Bye, Miss O'Donnell.

[ROBBIE *says loudly to Miss O'Donnell while she is walking away:*] Pimples go away, face herpes don't!

Boy King

Chris Quintos

REX, early 20s

REX *is talking with his friend.*

REX   Here's why I don't think I'm stringing Beth along. She absolutely knows that I don't want to get married right now. We talk about it all the time. Like all the time. Plus, Beth's a big girl. And she gets that I think it's a hack of a cultural convention. I mean, come on. We get married, have an outdated ceremony where we promise insane things to each other. She has an entourage of her "marryable friends" walk an entourage of my "marryable friends" down an aisle in an archaic procession in a white dress—that clearly symbolizes her virginity. I give her father five of my best camels that evening. Then what? On our wedding night, the king can have her first? [*Laughs.*]

If she has a problem with it—she'll bring it up. In fact, she has. And at the end of our conversations, she always sees what I'm saying. If not, she wouldn't be with me anymore, you know. THIS is my thing. THIS is my deal breaker. I won't do it. I've said that from the get-go. I'm not going to do something I don't believe in a hundred percent. But, I'm here. I'm committed. I love her. Why don't we just live in the moment. What we have is so great. Why change it? I love her so much, and she knows that.

Look, she's not like other girls. She's secure in what we have. She doesn't need convincing. Trust me, we've talked about it like a million times. In fact, we were out with her obnoxious cousin, Tracy, for brunch a couple of weeks ago. Tracy was newly engaged and asked when we would be. And Beth just told her—we aren't that kind of couple. And Tracy was like, what kind of couple, the marrying kind? And Beth was super cool and level headed and said—we just don't really believe in the institution. And if Tracy can't respect that, then let's just agree to disagree. And she shut the conversation down right there. She used the exact same arguments I've been using. It was awesome.

Irritable Male Syndrome

Lynn Trickey

RICHARD, 30s

A few guys sit around drinking beer, watching a football game.
RICHARD cheers a good play, then he casually starts chatting with
his buddies.

RICHARD   Hey, uh, you guys, you ever hear about this Male
PMS thing?

Yeah, I know—it's probably bullshit, huh?

[*Shouting at the TV.*]

Go! Go! Go! GO! Fuck, that should have been a first down.

My buddy was saying that he heard on NPR that men are on
cycles just like women. I guess it makes sense…you know, your
body has other cycles—breathing, nervous system—hell, your
cells replace themselves…every single cell replaces itself every
seven years. That's a cycle, right?

OH FUCK NO, REF! Come on! That's fucking bullshit! Are
you blind?!

Angie and I got in this fight last night over comforters.
Comforters! It was so stupid but I just couldn't help it I got so

mad. And then, as we're yelling at each other she accuses me of being a baby, and that really hurt you know? And I don't know why, but I just started to tear up and I couldn't stop!

COME ON!

Anyway I started reading about this: Irritable Male syndrome. This doctor said you can get frustrated, anxious, or just be really sensitive, and it's "associated with biochemical changes, hormonal fluctuations, stress, and loss of male identity."

What the fuck does that even mean? Loss of male identity. I know who I am. Just because I get upset when people say mean and hurtful things to me doesn't mean I'm overly sensitive.

And so what if it is related to my hormones? Everyone's got them, you know? And I let Angie eat her chocolate and I rub her tummy when she has cramps so maybe it's okay if I feel shitty once a month too.

[*He stands up, screaming.*]

COME ON, REF! GIVE THE GUY A FUCKING BREAK!
HE'S DOING HIS BEST. HE'S NOT GONNA BE
PERFECT. HE'S JUST A MAN FOR GODDSAKE!

[*He looks at his cohorts, composes himself. Sits back down.*]

Bullshit.

Office Blues

Matt Taylor

DAVID MARSH, early 30s

DAVID *spent a decade in the United States Marine Corps before leaving at the age of 30. He soon found work as a salesman for a large stationary company and often finds himself having to listen to the endless complaints of Sean Walsh, a dour, self-entitled twenty-something he shares a small cubicle with when he is working out of the office. The pair get along well enough, but* DAVID *is constantly exasperated by Sean's consistent complaints and often mocks him for his grim "the world is against me" demeanor.*

DAVID   Yeah, I'm alright, thanks Sean.

Ever since I left the Marines, I have a hard time feeling sorry for myself just because it's another regular Monday morning at the office.

I was in for almost a decade, yeah. I actually completed two full tours of Afghanistan. The first one involved doing nothing more than walking up and down some hills for six months, and the most dangerous thing my unit encountered was a donkey. Unfortunately, I went back for my second tour a few years later and I almost got blown to bits while I sat on the toilet.

And I really did, yeah; a rocket landed about twenty feet away from me while I was taking a dump.

Actually, it was good timing on their part, because when I shit myself in fear I was perfectly placed to get rid of my bodily waste. It would have been much more embarrassing if I had shit myself while I was eating breakfast or chatting with a policeman or something.

Apparently that's what happens during an insurgency, though. The enemy pack up all their shit and go on an extended fishing holiday when they know the whole military machine is en route. Then they just wait until the troops have started to get scaled back and everyone is getting bored and the next thing you know ten thousand enraged fighters are trying to chop you into bits because they think God likes that kind of behavior.

It's funny—they never seem to run out of suicide bombers, either, as you would think that they might struggle to find employees for that sort of job. They must have a PR team that would put Apple's to shame, because the mad fuckers fly into Afghanistan from all around the world just to volunteer for human-bomb duty. I never understood it until I met some of the locals and they told me that they were prohibited from drinking alcohol and everyone had more than one wife, and then it made perfect sense. If I had four fucking mothers-in-law and I was never allowed a beer, I'd probably be happy to scatter myself across a battlefield as well.

Honestly, if I went on patrol a hundred times during my second tour, I got shot at on ninety-nine of them. And after it was so quiet the first time around, I was a bit pissed off that I was actually going to be fighting for my life and not simply working on my tan again. Fortunately, the Taliban's training school isn't as efficient as its PR department, because the vast majority of them couldn't hit a cow's arse with a shovel let alone put a bullet in you from three hundred yards. Plus, you aren't standing still when people are shooting at you, either; you are running for cover like your life depends on it—and obviously it fucking does, because someone is trying to fill you full of holes with an AK-47.

So yeah anyway, it's not so bad sitting in an air-conditioned office, man, even if the money sucks and the manager is a bit of a dick, at least you can use the bathroom without fear of ending up shy a leg or an arm. Try and think on what I said the next time we run out of creamer or you get pissed off because the air-conditioning is playing up. There are plenty of worse places to be than here, even if you have to share a room with a miserable bastard like me.

So...are you going to pass me that stapler or are you worried I'm going to have a flashback and bludgeon you to death with it?

A True Gentleman

Leah Mann

THE GENTLEMAN, 30s

THE GENTLEMAN, *beefy with too much hair gel, wearing slacks and a shiny button down shirt that's looking worse for the wear, sprawls on a hard bench against the wall of the cell. He watches another guy piss in the corner.*

THE GENTLEMAN   Shit, man, what'd you eat? Oh, asparagus? Yeah, I heard about that smelly pee thing. Something chemical, right? My piss is probably like straight beer right now. I outta bottle that shit up, right? Sell it to hipsters on tap—locally made and shit. Ha-ha.

[*Beat.*]

Fuck, my head hurts. They ain't got a medicine cabinet or coffee hiding anywhere? Man, I been in jail before, but the drunk tank—this be a first for me.

[*Beat.*]

Ain't even my fault! Just tryin' to be a gentleman and have a good time and shit. Like women don't want you to be a man no more.

[*Beat.*]

I'm dating this girl, and tonight was our third date and out of nowhere she's just in a shit mood and jumping all over everything I say. So then I'm trying to be nice and calm her down, right?

[*Beat.*]

I just wanna have fun. It's my night off, I got some cash in my pocket, a beautiful girl on my arm...So it's raining, which I don't know how long you been in this windowless box here so maybe you don't know but it's been raining for like three days—but it's that misty rain that makes the streets pretty like in those old movies.

[*Beat.*]

She's wearing heels and a dress so I'm being polite—I keep moving around so I'm on the outside and she won't get splashed or hurt or nothing. That's manners, man. I offer her my coat, she says she don't need it. But I know she's cold in that dress so I give her my coat even though she says she don't want it. Then we get to this bar but we're going to this secret room in the back and she ain't never been there. Well I'm all like, ladies first, ladies first...you know that shit, women love?

[*Beat.*]

And out of fucking nowhere she blows up at me. She pushes me in front because "she don't know where she's going and it's not polite, it's just annoying for me to be herding her along like a sheep when it'd be so much easier for me to just walk in front since I know where the secret door is and she didn't want my coat so why don't I listen to her. She's not a liar, if she says she isn't cold she isn't cold and it's disrespectful to be pushy like that and she's not a child either and doesn't need help walking down the fucking street—she's been walking down the street by herself her whole life and she's not looking for a nanny or some man who thinks she's like some pathetic, helpless little girl."

[*Beat.*]

And I'm standing there like what the hell is happening right now because I'm just treating her like a lady, like my mama taught me, and she's going on about being objectified and how I don't even see her as a real, actual, individual human being but that she's just some girl whose feelings and thoughts are irrelevant to how I act towards her and then tears off my coat and puts it over my shoulders like I'm a girl—which was pretty fuckin' funny because she's like a foot shorter than me and was trying to make this dramatic point but she could barely reach high enough to get the coat on my shoulders without it falling off—and then she spins around and is like, "What, you aren't gonna open the door for me? 'Cause apparently my tits mean my arms don't work as well as a man's." And she's gone.

[*Beat.*]

Yeah. Seriously. So I go into the secret bar in back all by myself because at least I still got cash in my pocket—more now that I'm not buying this girl drinks. I'm sitting at the bar with my beer and there's this couple in a booth, pretty good looking and you can tell the girl is bored, like whatever this dude is saying is only funny in his head but she's trying to be nice and every time he pauses she tries to change the subject or say something and he just talks over her—meanwhile he's touching her hair and getting her free drinks.

[*Beat.*]

And that shit makes me think. You know, like really think about what my girl had been saying and how I treat girls.

[*Beat.*]

I mean right there—"girls." She's a grown-ass woman. She got a job and pay her own bills and take care of herself and she's right, she don't need help walking down the street. I start thinking about the little things I been saying and doing without realizing what they mean, you know, how they be taken by the other person and fuck if it don't turn out I'm an asshole. I ain't no white knight or gentleman 'cause I treated them all the same even though they different people and that's all she was saying. It's not about her tits or ass or ovaries or whatever—I mean those are great for certain activities but she want to be a *person*.

[*Beat.*]

My mind is all blown, I mean, shit, I just blew my own mind! Deep fucking epiphany and self-realization.

[*Beat.*]

I'm all amped up and then that couple from the booth gets up and I'm behind them 'cause I got a plan. I'm gonna go to that girl's house like in the movies and be standing in the rain and tell her she was right and I get it now and to give me another chance and I won't never condescend or nothing to her again.

[*Beat.*]

So the dude from this couple pushes in front of the girl to open the door for her so she has to stand there and wait while he does it and she's rolling her eyes, I can see it. So I'm like, "Bro, don't open the door for her, she's a grown-up, she got it." He

gets up in my face for being rude and he's just being a
gentleman and it ain't my business anyways.

[*Beat.*]

One thing led to another and here I am. Drunk and disorderly.

[*Beat.*]

He ain't such a man he can take a punch; I guess holding doors
is easier.

[*Beat.*]

Course I also pissed on him, which was definitely not polite or
mature. But it's all good, because I'm using this time in here
smelling your asparagus pee and the puke to think about what
being a man means and soon as I'm out I'm buying that girl a
hot new dress and a gourmet dinner to prove I'm a changed
man. Girls love that shit.

Project Disaster

Chris Quintos

JAVIER, mid-20s to mid-30s

JAVIER *is a contestant on a Project Runway–like reality TV show.*

JAVIER   WHAT IN THE HOLY SWEET MOTHER OF
EFF IS KENDRA MAKING? WHAT. IS. SHE. MAKING?!?!
Is it a dress? Is it a skirt? Is it a plane?

[JAVIER *makes an Incorrect buzz sound.*]

It's a visual affront. That's what it is. It's Rude. With a capital *R*.
I mean, it's like if a starving, blind monkey ravaged a bag of
Cheetos, but, like, ugly. RIGHT? Am I alone in thinking that?
God, if only the whole thing was Cheetos Orange, I think
Kendra would be in a better place. I mean, orange IS the new
black. But blah-blah brown and drab green trim? What was she
thinking? She clearly wasn't. I mean—the emperor can't design
clothes! The emperor can't even pick a good textile! Hello! Oh
my god. I could talk about that monstrosity all day. Rude.
Capital *R-U-D-E*. I know I shouldn't—

[*To producer.*]

This is going to make me look terrible, isn't it? Sorry, Mom! I
love you! I swear I'm still a good person! Mom knows I like to
talk. Sorry, Twitterverse! Well, the part of Twitter that doesn't
appreesh the fast-talking truth. #Rude. Whatever.

But like, for real—the dress!!! Or what I shall lovingly refer to as "The Sack of Sad." Kendra has made that poor tiny beautiful model's body look like a lumpy bag of hemp protein powder in the sale aisle of the health food store no one goes to anymore. Hemp powder is out, Kendra! #Duh. It's tragic, really. I mean, Kendra actually *has* a woman's body; you'd think she might know how to make it look good! (I mean, I don't have one, yet I manage to do fine.)

[*Winks at camera.*]

Do you know any woman who wants MORE attention paid to her hips? I don't! Not even Shakira wants that. And Shakira's hips don't lie. And the makeup—MY GOD. I know she was going for "sailor chic meets Bowie"—but it's more like "sailor freak meets no one"...because she's ugly. Rude, I say. *R-U-D-E.* Rude. That dress is rude. Follow me! @JaviSlays

Barry Franklin

Andy Goldenberg

BARRY, 20s to 40s

BARRY, *a nerd of the highest order, confronts his coworker, Gary, who has been spreading nasty rumors about him around the office.*

BARRY   Gary, I want to talk to you about the rumors you've been spreading about me around the office. ~~No, they're rumors.~~ They're vicious, and they hurt me. You keep telling people that I've never had sex, which I did say to you…in confidence… but you didn't let me finish. Yes, I have never had sex—while skydiving. I had the chance. Twice. With this girl. Just a girl.

Can't even remember her name. I mean, I guess she was hot by supermodel standards. But for a supermodel, she was super jealous of all my girlfriends. My friends who were girls. But I HAVE had girlfriends who were more than friends. I've just never had a girlfriend—that wasn't sex crazed.

They're all starving for sex. You know? So I give it to them. Because you have to give them what they want, right? Girls, right? But there's no feelings involved. I mean, I wish there were, you know? I want to settle down soon, start a family. I can't just keep going out to dance clubs and house parties until two or three in the morning if I want to make partner. And I don't want to let down my favorite girl friend, my mom. If I can be totally honest Gary, a woman has never touched me like my mom. What's so funny? Oh come on Gary. Grow up! You know what I mean! I do not have sex with my mom! Gary!

Hold It In

JP Karliak

KALEB, early 20s to mid-30s

At a vegan kosher Jewish/Buddhist deli in Harlem, KALEB meets up with his very best friend from college, Tom. Wait, no, it's Bill. Let's just settle on Marcus. So Marcus has just shared that he's popped the question to his longtime girlfriend Cynthia. But KALEB is more interested in his personal creative blockage. And the freedom that it brings.

KALEB Wow. Getting married. I think that's incredible, man. No, seriously, you and Cynthia have been a long time coming. Wow. You guys at my concert, back when I was testing my acoustic work, not the overproduced wagon of crap of old. And the connection you guys had, I could see it from the stage—it had a ripeness, an aroma almost. I'm glad I could bring you together.... Well, maybe you'd been dating, but your relationship leveled up from my music. I wish it wasn't so effective at relationship building—I'd feel less burdened. Shit, that was such a dark period. For me. You know, the album failure, cranking out creativity like it's ground chuck.

But we all pass through darkness. Big, unexpected carwashes of feces. They follow me. I feel like a massive drain of creative nothingness awaits me in every random Laundromat and gastropub. Case in point, I was shopping for juice cleanses the other day... because let's speak truth, if you buy just any squeezed fruit, you might as well start an IV drip of Sunny D into your veins. So much phony dreck out there. And I'm doing my research at this new place in the Flatiron District. Juice is good, but proximity to Shake Shack makes me die a little inside…that thing became corporate like a cancer, man, like a fucking wildfire. And, lo, one of my songs comes on in the store. That one that the Decemberists swear they wrote, but was really mine? And I had to flee. Ran home. Which is forty blocks, and not easy in my slip-ons, let me notate that, but I ran the whole way because I felt in my gut how fleeting creativity can be.

Everyone preaches "What you create is yours, it's your art, nobody can ever take away from you what you give birth to," which is such bullshit, as you well know as an artist.…Well, when you used to draw whatever that propaganda was back in college.…"Graphic design," sure, label as you will. But the thing is, anybody can drain whatever they want out of you. I mean, fuck, we ask for it, practically falling all over ourselves to get our dick sucked or a Groupon for a colon cleanse, right? I know, who uses Groupon anymore? It's such a scam. I just think that the only thing we can really keep is the stuff that we don't put out there. Prolificness is a joke that a capitalist society makes you believe is so vital, if for nothing else but to have a new title on Kindle or in Costco, but look at Harper fucking Lee! You think anything beyond *To Kill a Mockingbird* would have been as good? Hypothetically, she writes *To Maim a Red-Breasted Robin*, gets a fat check, gets ripped apart by critics, and a little more of her soul dies. Fuck that! And even writing that first book probably ruined her. And the movie? I'd have more respect for her if I had no idea who the hell she was. There is a second book? Oh God, she should have Sylvia Plath'd herself.

I say internalize your work. It's not creative constipation—it's holding down your food and not vomiting on cue like some trained bulimic monkey. The creative energy within is what makes me, me, and you, you, right? It's what allows us to sit here as friends and just commiserate. I don't have to tell you, but you know if I really put myself out there, I could be on the *Billboard* Top 10 or the *New York Times* Best Sellers list. It's not hard—it's just feeding into whatever fast-food flavor of the week the masses want, right? But who would I be after it's done? Would I be compassionate? Would I have the best in mind for humanity? And I don't mean spokesmodeling for some overhyped charity that does nothing for the starving kids in Africa, parading them around like puppets. Besides, their hunger, my hunger, your hunger, it's all equal in way. And not to be iconoclastic here, but I think I feel that hunger more than those kids, which is maybe why I feel this concept so acutely. I can't keep enough creative energy in my bowels to keep myself fed. Every interaction, every sentence I speak is giving up a little of me. I was at Mount Sinai last week for exhaustion, did you know that? It's a wonder I don't collapse every fucking day. But you know what it's like, you've put yourself out there, you gave your heart to this girl and now you're getting a divorce.... Right, married.... Okay, really, is there a difference? Each a big three-ring circus of how much or how little you care for somebody? It sounds exhausting. Trust me, emote as little as possible, hold it in like oxygen and you'll be the last who needs to come up for air. Just last week, my therapist said that I had too much empathy at my job at CVS, so I quit.

Vaguely related tangent—you can grab the check, right?

On a Bended, Bruised, Battered, and Broken Knee
(or How Not to Not Propose Marriage to My Daughter)

Jeff Bogle

JEFF, 52

JEFF is the father of two girls in their early 20s. He is speaking to a boy in the foyer of his house, a nonroom of constant flux, while one of his daughter is upstairs getting changed (again).

JEFF Listen, while she's upstairs changing clothes again. We have some time to talk.... Future son-in-law, I need to save you from yourself. Listen up...

It may surprise you that for many women, still, to this day, regardless of the strides made in equality and the women's liberation movement as first spearheaded by the tireless singsong efforts of a sashed Mrs. Banks in Mary Poppins's England, the idea of being proposed to, by a man and on bended knee, remains one of life's most eagerly awaited occasions.

How will he do it? When will he do it? Where will he do it?

The Hollywood rom-com industry is built, in part, upon these eternal questions. Cast Patrick Dempsey in the lead, and shazam! Another summer blockbuster tailor-made for girls' night out. Who's bringing the wine?

You should know that there's nothing else in the world that blends, so seamlessly, both the commonplace and the cinematic quite like the wedding proposal. You can probably already picture it: handsome and earnest you, on single knee, her hand in yours, your eyes to the heavens, the sun setting behind her back, her face as a silhouette, her mouth agasp.

Your parochial wonder in that exact moment of bliss is only found in a boy whose heart is free of emotional shrapnel.

People once got excited about going to war, too.

And I get it, I do, that instant when boy asks girl and girl says yes is a time and a place that will be filed away in a woman's own personal Library of Congress, archived away with her first kiss, first baseball game with dad, first pint of ice-cream after that first bad breakup, first nonfaked orgasm. This all means that you should try really extra-super-duper-hard not to screw it up. Because shit memories are cataloged too, and a misstep on the marriage proposal tip will haunt you 'til the end of days.

Trust me.

My old girl and I worked at the same financial services company throughout much of the opening salvo of our relationship. Ours was a classic story: we were young, we were in love, we were cash poor, and we were bank tellers surrounded by twenty-dollar bills. We were the most boring adaption of Bonnie and Clyde ever conceived. We'd met at that bank on the corner of Second and South Street in Philadelphia, the exact spot of which, I should tell you now, is a toilet inside an organic ice-cream joint, a fact that I swear is a metaphor for exactly nothing. While we first conjugated our love in the land of cheesesteaks and soft pretzels, we quickly followed each other out to the 'burbs for a fresher start and for fatter paychecks. After the first couple of weeks of being together, it was a foregone conclusion we'd someday tie the knot. But I was never a Boy Scout—I couldn't tie shit together properly. When it came time to eventually get married, after we'd eradicated our baggage, like her ex-boyfriend who was still living in her parent's house and my credit card debt, which played the role of my ex-boyfriend, I had to propose. I guessed. I was never any good at kindergarten sequencing. She was, she was better, and she assured me that yes, the proposal picture comes first. We had a date and location picked out but we weren't technically, in the eyes of the law or prim and proper society or her family and friends or not even me, engaged to be wed.

Thankfully, I had a plan, the perfect plan. Airtight.

I'd whisk her away to Detroit (seriously) and I'd get down on bended knee and officially ask her to be my wife on the steps of Joe Louis Arena, the home of my beloved Red Wings Hockey Club (seriously). Because, I figured, if I had to do it, I would insert a bit of my own fantasy into the situation. That seemed only fair, by WWPDD Law; that is exactly what Patrick Dempsey would do, too. I mean, yes, he would probably gallop down Steve Yzerman Drive on a horse, but still, close enough.

Conveniently enough, I was already scheduled to travel to Detroit for business reasons, and my girl, she was going to be my companion during the trip. With my own airfare, hotel, and car rental covered by the company we worked for, all we needed to do was splurge on a flight for her and tickets to a Red Wings game, both of which were booked solid. Like I said, airtight.

With that locked down, it was time to lock down my fiancé. Not literally, of course. She wasn't into that. Still isn't, despite my assertions that I will not lose the keys. But a funny thing happened on the way to the arena. My brilliant fallen-American-city-hockey-stadium-wedding-proposal scheme? Yeah, it didn't quite come off. What did happen was this:

The client canceled the trip. No one was going to Detroit. Most people would be high-fiving about missing a trip to that depressing, crumbling-even-then American city. Me? Not so much. I was catatonic. When we met for lunch later that day in the company's airplane hanger–sized cafeteria, I was despondent. She couldn't understand why, obviously—she wasn't hip to what I had in store for her and she wouldn't quit asking why this was bothering me so much. Yeah, we'd miss a hockey game, she said. We'll catch one later down the line, she said. No biggie, she said. To her it seemed I was code red over missing a stupid regular season hockey game. Which, had that been all we'd be missing out on, would have been idiot, yes. But you know now what she didn't then, that this was way more than a hockey game. What was more idiotic than my psychotic behavior was what I finally said to her. Yeah. No kidding.

In a moment I will never live down, in a moment stored away until the end of days, a moment I'd like you to try hard to imagine so as not to make the same mistake I did, I told her that I was *going* to propose to her. In Detroit. At the Red Wings game. Oh but I didn't just tell her, oh no, I yelled it at her, in the middle of our company's cafeteria, in the middle of lunchtime, as if she was to blame for the client putting the kibosh on my master plan.

Of the many sentences a man can mutter aloud to a woman he loves with a mouth full of turkey club sandwich, "I was GOING TO propose to you" is, without a doubt, the dumbest.

And that, son, is how not to propose marriage to the woman you love.

So, you best get it together, Junior, and rent the entire Patrick Dempsey oeuvre, stat. Come to think of it, now might be the ideal time to learn how to saddle up a horse, too. You've gotta give my daughter the fairytale proposal scene she deserves…otherwise, she'll archive away your stupidity and make you wear it like a sash for the rest of your life.

Twinsies!

Evolution of Masturbating

Kenny Madrid

CARL, 40

CARL *has just realized he's no longer young, because his teenaged son was just caught doing something that used to be taboo for him at that age, but now he does with reckless abandon, because whatever...his wife's not giving him any. It takes place in his living room, the most open area for someone to be caught masturbating, and his son, 16, has had enough time with himself (so to speak) to not care about the risk of being caught.*

CARL   Son, I know you have grown up in a time where the Internet is a fact. There was no time for you that existed before the Internet, which is a scary and monumental achievement for all of mankind. The Internet has brought us closer together in ways my parents and grandparents could not have imagined. Sure it has its problems, but it also has unlimited possibilities to spread good around the world. So the fact that I caught you nonchalantly masturbating to several videos at the same time, on almost every screen in the house, is quite startling for me. Masturbating to porn wasn't always so easy in my day. Now, don't try to interrupt, this could get graphic.

Sure, you could lay in your room and use your imagination to picture two women making out while you take turns plowing the two, but we aren't all Pablo Picasso and can paint beautiful and strange portraits of boobs out of thin air. Most of us need some kind of visual aid.

My first case of self-pleasuring came so early in life, I can't even recall it. One night in my senior year of high school, I had my girlfriend of several months over to eat dinner with my family, my dad, mom, and sister. For reasons I won't get into now, we shall refer to her as Beelzebub. Though Beelzebub was no stranger to my family, it was the first time she had sat down to dinner with all of us. My family took this opportunity to recount every moment that could possibly embarrass me: the time I accidentally kicked myself in the face and broke my nose, peeing my pants at baseball camp, breaking my wrist after chest bumping my dad. But the kicker was when they revealed to Beelzebub that during my sister's countless dance practices and recitals, I would hump things. When I say things, apparently it was whatever object was closest to my wiener. Something I could press up against rapidly and furiously. My first masturbation experiences involved dance squads practicing their routines while I stood in the corner and pushed my baby penis against a couch. Beelzebub later told me the story made perfect sense. "You're a humper," she explained. Thanks, parents. They weren't cool like me, they were dicks.

My first *sentient* case of masturbating came from the monthly Victoria's Secret catalogs that would come in the mail and "mysteriously" disappear along with the occasional *People* magazine featuring anything with Carmen Electra in it. Let me take a step back. Magazines are like those books that nobody touches in those buildings called libraries we see people in the movies studying in. Victoria's Secret didn't even sell anything as risqué as thong underpants at the time. Tame by today's standards (you can see more on HBO or even FX nowadays). But still, the women were beautiful, and my hormonal fireworks were ready to light up the Fourth of July. Of breasts. Those magazines would give me satisfaction for the entire month, sometimes longer if I couldn't get my hands on them before my mom did. It did not occur to me until telling you this how messed up masturbating to the pictures of women wearing the clothes my mom might ultimately purchase really is.

The next discovery on my long list of masturbation sources was my discovery of channel 96. Now, televisions did not always connect to a cable box. Cable cords went directly into the television and you turned the channel up and down, as opposed to today where the television never changes channels, everything is worked through the cable box. During this caveman period of watching television, channels only went up to 99. I'm sure most areas varied, but for my house channels 75 through 99 were nothing but static, or "snow" as many called it. There was rarely a reason to view those stations, until one glorious day when I discovered a scrambled porn station on channel 96. I don't understand how most things work in this world, so I'll save you the terrible explanation of why stations get scrambled, but needless to say it looked like the She-Hulk had gone into porn. Once in a while, it would unscramble enough and I could make out a breast or two, or something even more scandalous. Like a butthole. This posed a huge problem for someone as young as myself at the age of ten. My parents never wanted to leave me at home by myself, constantly fearing home invasions, child rapists, and toy parts I could swallow. Occasionally, I would convince them to leave me alone if I promised that I would be fine. That is, if "fine" meant watching scrambled porn. Or I would be brave enough to watch it and hope that I would hear whoever was about to turn the corner and change the channel before they entered the room. Keep in mind, I was still in my stage of only being able to hump and push against things. Much easier to disguise why I'm hunched over a couch than if my hand was down my pants. Eventually, this grew too dangerous to maintain, but luckily for me, my parents plugged our computer into the Internet for the first time entering a whole new era of masturbation.

At first, my Internet use was fairly G-rated. I would play simple 2-D computer games, type up reports, and browse through *Encyclopædia Britannica* CDs. Like a good little child. One day, a friend introduced me to KaZaA, a crude version of a torrent site. When I say crude, I mean a three-minute video could take days to download. Makes the "I'm horny and need porn right now" situation a little more difficult. What if you had downloaded an Asian girl masturbating but were in the mood for anal penetration? It was anarchy. Preparation was required. I started off slow with a lot of music downloads, you know, the reason why the music industry is failing. Every once in a while with much deliberation, I would search "Britney Spears naked." It would come up with a series of fake, naked pictures of Britney Spears. At the time "Hit Me Baby One More Time" had come out, there was nothing better than Britney. I escalated quickly to searching the dirtiest things I could think of, like "boobs," "breasts," "titties," and even "paginas." (Side note: No, I wasn't searching for the Spanish-to-English translation of "paginas." When I was little, a friend had told me that a girl's private parts is called a pagina. Why wouldn't I believe Matthew? He had been my best friend for over a year and had never pushed me off of a slide.) Though searching on KaZaA was a perilous task: there were no preview pictures, only titles. A video could be downloaded after days of waiting and end up a video some guy's penis who had pranked all of these unwitting kids. Again, not realizing how messed up this is until I just typed this out. Keeping in mind that I was doing all of this on our family computer, I continued at a rate of near exhaustion for both my computer and my penis until one day my mom asked me why her e-mail inbox was full of deals for porn. I had never given out her e-mail, or any e-mail for that matter, but clearly that doesn't keep malware from doing their thing.

For a few years of high school my porn habits stayed dormant, knowing that I could not continue to wreck my family computer all in the hope of seeing breasts every once in a while. The Internet was still fresh enough that there was no centralized area to view porn. You had to risk getting a virus nearly every time you downloaded porn. And forget streaming, YouTube was in its infancy. Besides, dial-up Internet was so slow that any streaming service out there would buffer every two seconds. Nothing takes me out of the story of a porno more than buffering. But on my eighteenth birthday, I finally set foot inside of an adult video store. It was awful. I hated it. There were dildos so massive I immediately questioned whether I had lost the better part of my penis during circumcision. (Side note: I'm average. No girl has ever been stoked or appalled at the size, just so we're all aware). The Paris Hilton sex tape was on sale. For ninety-five dollars! This seemed entirely outrageous to me. After I purchased the items on my younger friends' shopping list, I left, vowing to never return. I was thankful I didn't see any adults other than the store clerks.

In college, there was not much need for porn because of the crazy parties going on. That's not to say I was sleeping with a lot of (or any) girls, but many nights girls would be walking around topless. It was like interactive theater. But for porn. Moaning could be heard in the halls every single night as I would sit in my room watching Judd Apatow movies, thinking "Who has sex on a Monday?" Still, there was plenty live material to work with until the day a friend revealed to me the plethora of porn sites that don't require download, credit card information, or effort of any kind. Sites like YouPorn, PornHub, and XVideos brought porn viewing into the twenty-first century. It was as if I opened a treasure chest and the gold bitcoins from inside shined in my face. Only the gold was actually, tits. Most boys grow up masturbating but I was one of the few that graduated from one platform to the next as the porn technology did. It's a confusing time for anyone at that age, but thank God I had good friends and either a completely naive family, or just one that gave up after they found me humping a couch at the age of three.

Now son, I'm going to leave you alone because you seem to still have your penis in your hand, and that kind of tenacity should be rewarded.

You know I'll always be proud of you, just not with this.

Now, if you'll excuse me—your good ole dad needs to get on the Internet.

College Dad

Carla Cackowski

DOTING DAD, 50s

A DOTING DAD *is caught by his daughter walking out of her college dormitory with a laundry basket in his hands.*

DOTING DAD   Oh, hey sweetheart! Ma asked me to swing by and pick up your laundry. No, I know you have machines on campus. I just thought, well your mother thought, that maybe you'd forget to separate colors from whites and that you'd try to put your blouses in the dryer and then they'd shrink and then, before you know it, me and your ma have to take our college freshman shopping for new clothes all over again.

[*Sets basket down.*]

No, you're right honey. I'm sorry. One of us should've called you first to tell you I was coming. We just didn't want to distract you from your studies, or from making new friends, or any other activities you've been up to lately. So, what activities have you been up to lately? Not much? That doesn't sound very "first semester" exciting to me! But seriously, what've you been up to?

Hmm? Oh. Your RA let me in. Well, she knew I was your father. Don't you remember introducing us when we dropped you off? No need to get upset with her, sweetheart. She let me in because I told her I had to drop off your meds. [*Whispers.*] Don't worry, she's not going to tell anyone. Of course you don't take meds, I know you don't take meds, you're my daughter for goodness sakes, I know you're not on medication, but I just needed her to let me in so your mother and I could surprise you by stealing your clothes—borrowing your clothes—to clean them, and we didn't think she would let us in for that reason alone. So, in order to justify my entering your dorm room when you weren't here, I told her I was dropping off your medication. Clonazepam. It's not embarrassing. I'm on that medication, as is your mother. So? So that means there's a good chance you'll be on antianxiety meds once you have kids too. No. It is not embarrassing.

You're right. I'm sorry. My apologies. Our apologies. Your mother and I apologize. We are just worried about you. You haven't called and, before you know it, the semester will be over and we just—I mean, we are paying for your education for goodness sakes, and to not hear from you since we dropped you off! It's only been two days? Can that be right? No, you're right. You are right. Huh. Well…two days is a very long time. Legally, we could've filed a missing person's report after one day, we gave you a whole extra day, and you still didn't call to check in!

Sweetheart, I understand. You've been busy. Of course. We understand. Your mother and I understand. Just call us each night until we've gotten used to you being on your own, okay? Thank you. And you can always call us in the morning too— Just a thought! Once a day. Fine.

No, you don't need to call your mother right now. I'll tell her you said hi. No, sweetheart, don't call your mother right now.

Please don't call your mother. No—Okay, fine! Truth time. Your mother doesn't know I'm here. Technically. But! She would've wanted me to check in with you. Fine! But please don't tell her that I broke into your dorm room. I mean, please don't tell her your RA let me into your window—uh, door! Your door. [*Sighs.*] I should go home now. It's a two-hour drive, you know? Talk to you tomorrow. Night-night, sweetheart. Lock the door behind me.

[DAD *turns to leave*—]

And the window. You know not to let anyone in after 11:00 p.m., right? Even your roommate. She shouldn't be coming in that late, she could be on drugs, she could be dangerous—okay! Leaving now! Love you.

Goodbye, Grandpa Joe

Jessica Glassberg

SID, 40s

SID, *nervous, wearing a consignment store black suit, addresses his family at the reading of his grandfather's will.*

SID   Hello. Hi, everyone. Okay…I wish we were all meeting under better circumstances, but here we are…I will now be reading the Last Will and Testament of Joseph Marvin Flick. Let us take a moment to remember that Grandpa Joe loved you all.

[*A Beat. Then, reading.*]

"I, Joseph Marvin Flick never loved anyone."

[*There is a beat as* SID *awkwardly smiles at his family. He continues reading.*]

"Sure, I got to give it to some ladies in my day. And I ended up in the family way with the woman you called Me-maw and I called Fat Ruth. Surprise Sid, you were a mistake. We had three more beasts and all our beasts had their own beasts and now I'm dead and you hairy beasts want all my stuff."

[SID *notices people getting upset.*]

Michelle. Come on, no, he's not talking about your chin hairs. You know he was starting to lose it towards the end.

[*Reading.*]

"I don't want anyone saying I was losing my mind, or wasn't thinking straight. I'm straight as an arrow as I dictate this. Straighter than that tutti fruitcake of a grandson. The one singing them show tunes. Bill, or Jim, or whatever his name is...or was...maybe someone mistook his singing for the sound of an animal dying and he was finally put out of his misery."

[SID *addresses his nephew.*]

He didn't mean it, Johnny. No one thinks you're...ya know. And if you were, we'd love ya just the same. Well, not that same way Grandpa Joe was talking about; we'd be more accepting of your lifestyle choices...You have the voice of an angel.

[*Then...*]

Let's get back on track. Where was I?

[*Reading.*]

"...he was finally put out of his misery. Hope you're not sweating too much up there, Sid. I asked that Sid read this because I know how much he hates public speaking and I figured it'd be good for him to finally grow some balls."

[SID, *to family.*]

Okay...I have balls. Obviously, I have balls. I have two beautiful children. Sorry that you had to hear your father say "balls" twice...three times. And they are mine. My kids...not my balls. Well, technically they're all mine. I made my kids using my ba...testicles. Look at Kacie's ears.

[*To his daughter.*]

Sorry sweetheart, you got my Dumbos. But they look much better on you. Ya know what? It's okay, Grandpa Joe is still the guy you all remember. The guy who could drink beer from sunup till sundown and still beat you at checkers. The guy who would be too drunk to play catch, or read us stories, or call us on our birthdays. The guy who'd beat us with his belt because he beat us at checkers. Who'd tell us we were "worse than manure. At least manure was good for something." The guy who didn't make it to my wedding because he said I wasn't worth marrying. I AM worth marrying. My wife loves me! She loves my big ears and my balls. Ya know what? I don't care what he left me. Margie, get the coats and I'll meet you and the kids at the car. Joseph Marvin Flick? More like Joseph Marvin Dick!

[SID *exits the stage. Beat. He marches back in.*]

Did he leave me the car?

Knock Knock

Mark Alderson

DERRICK, early 20s to mid-30s

DERRICK, *a young and anxious man, is standing outside of an apartment door talking to himself while holding a small bouquet of flowers.*

DERRICK   Why is this so difficult? All I have to do is knock. I mean, she said yes to the date, so why would I have to be nervous about picking her up? Do I smell okay? Should I have worn a jacket? You know, like one of those cool ones that says "I am confident but open to feedback." No, I don't need a jacket and I smell great. Here it goes.

Hmm, should I knock or use the doorbell? Knocking is a bit more gentlemen-like, but if I use the doorbell then I will be sure that she hears me. However, if I knock then I can do like, a cool rhythm and she will think that I will have awesome music abilities. But what happens when she asks about my musical talents and I say that I don't have any? Oh man, then she will think that I have been lying to her this whole time and it will all go to crap. No no no, it's all good. I am going to knock with a pleasant rhythm and she will think that I am a pleasant man.

[*Knock knock.*]

[*The apartment door opens and an old woman smoking a cigar answers, catching DERRICK off guard.*]

Umm. Hello? I am looking for Catherine Esplinade. Does she live here? Wrong door, you say? Well, that's unfortunate because that makes me now thirty seconds late.

[*The old woman blows a puff of smoke in* DERRICK'*s face and slams the door.*]

Hmm. Apartment 213. This must be it.

[DERRICK *knocks on the next door. A familiar face answers.*]

Jessica? Do you live here? It's me, Derrick. Um, you stood me up two weeks ago at Maloney's. Boy, that was a bummer. You never even called or texted me to say you weren't coming. I was really excited to go out with you. I guess it works out because after a few frozen margaritas, the bartender that night set me up with his cousin. So in your face! Actually, I'm sorry, that was mean, but I am on my way to pick her up right now. Do you know where apartment 213 is?

[*The door slams shut on the flowers and ruins them.* DERRICK *walks over to the next door with a limp bouquet of roses and knocks. A beautiful woman answers.*]

Oh my gosh it's finally you, Catherine. I've met so many different women tonight trying to get into your apartment. I mean, not like that—but sort of. I can tell you all about it over drinks. You don't drink on a first date? But you will on a second? Well that's uh, well that's weird. No, I don't mean *you're* weird but your rules need to be a bit looser. No I wasn't saying *you* need to be looser but you could give me a break. Look I even got you these flowers!

[*Catherine's door slams in his face.* DERRICK *walks swiftly and knocks on the second door. Jessica answers again.*]

Hey, I don't know if you believe in fate or anything, but you've got to admit that this is a bit serendipitous. You see, you're beautiful and I'm wondering if you'd like to give this thing a second chance? I am sure you had a great reason for not coming that night, I now know all about what can happen before I date. No pressure at all but I think if the universe gives you a second chance—well you've got to say yes. So are you free tonight?

What's that? Sure! I would be delighted to come back in twenty minutes to pick you up. Let me just write down your apartment number real quick so I don't get lost. Awesome. See you in twenty minutes. I hope you like frozen margaritas because I know just the place.

Climb On

Leah Mann

CALEB, 20s

Exterior snow covered rocky mountain. CALEB, 20s, lies with his leg trapped under a rock and snow swirling around him. He's wearing climbing gear, his face red from the cold.

CALEB   Whoa! You okay, man? Phew. That was some mother of a tumble! I'm over here! Under the snow behind this huge rock. Dude, I'd totally come to you but this boulder on my leg is not moving.

[*Grimaces.*]

Talk about gnarly, look at my leg! The part that isn't under the rock—crushed like a beer can. Is that bone? It's so thick.

[*Beat.*]

Bro, it's all good. Just push the boulder off and I'll totally be fine. It's just a leg. And you know what we say—no pain, no gain. ONE...TWO...THREE...THREE!!...Three, bro, three.

[*Beat.*]

Seriously? You can't push any harder than that? It didn't move at all. Weak.

[*Sighs.*]

No, not you. The situation.

[*Beat.*]

It's gonna get dark soon. Can you call for help on the radio?
No battery? We shouldn't have worn it down telling dick jokes
to that sherpa. Bad planning on our part, ha-ha. Looks like
we're stuck here until help comes.

[*Beat.*]

I'M stuck here? Technically, yes, I'm the one who's stuck, if
we're going to be literal. Are we being that literal?

[*Beat.*]

I guess you're right. I'm not trying to hold you back. That's not
how we roll. We've been friends, what? Since we were eight
and building skate ramps in your back yard?

[*Beat.*]

And sure, we swore a blood oath to always be there for each
other and blood is thicker than water, but it ain't thicker than
ice and I understand that this majestic frozen mountain we're
on is a once in a lifetime opportunity for you.

[*Beat.*]

You're so close…I totally get it. I'll be here when you descend
and you can bring help. Maybe steal one of those flags off the
top to use as a lever on this boulder. That's science.
Resourcefulness man.

[*Beat.*]

Of course I believe in taking responsibility for my actions.

[*Beat.*]

You're right. It's my own fault. I should have been more careful. Safety first. You shouldn't have to suffer the consequences of my mistakes. That'd be messed up. Like that time we cheated on the chem final and you threw me under the bus, that was messed up! And you felt like a jackass, bro, remember? Well, I don't want to feel like a jackass for holding you back. We're bigger than that now. This is totally my bad.

[*Beat.*]

This pain and the cold, that's life man. The danger is half the beauty of what we do. I got no regrets. Well, I regret not packing new rope. That was stupid. But lesson learned. Every step we take determines our next set of choices. Sometimes you can backtrack and try a new path, but some steps shut the door behind you. That toe hold, the patch of black ice, the old rope…that sent me down this path and I can't time travel, which is such a bummer because that would be dope.

[*Beat.*]

That's all the past and I'm about the now. This is my now. I'm embracing it, dude. My decisions, my consequences. The present is a gift, am I right? Now it's your turn to decide.

[*Beat.*]

Our universe has converged in this exact moment in space and time—in my life and in your life—and you have two options.

[*Beat.*]

ONE—You go. You climb this mountain like the athlete you are. You stand on the summit and feel the weight of your accomplishment under your feet, lifting you up into the sky. You breathe that frigid air on the top of the world and you look down at earth through the clouds with the gods for both of us.

[*Beat.*]

Or TWO, you stay with me until a rescue crew gets here. You make sure I don't go into shock and that there aren't any complications, that I don't get hypothermia—and NEITHER of us makes it to the summit. The whole trip is wasted and we return defeated and disappointed—but alive and hopefully not crippled! Which for me, would be nice because I'm pretty attached to using both my legs.

[*Beat.*]

Either way we will be bonded by this gnarly experience forever. So...will you stay or will you go?

[*Beat.*]

You'll go? Really?

[*Beat.*]

I'm guess I don't need BOTH legs. People make do, right? Give me your knife. I thought of a third option. I'm not gonna stand in the way of your dreams, I'm gonna stand next to you. We do this the way we started, together!

[*He starts sawing through the top of his thigh.*]

Don't want to cut it too close, know what I'm saying? Family jewels and all that. And...there go my new pants.

[*Beat.*]

My adrenaline is going crazy right now! This is what it's all about—looking challenges straight in the eye and punching them in the face!

[*Beat.*]

Oh shit, wrong leg.

[*He starts sawing on the other one with determination.*]

Got any more dick jokes? I have very muscular thighs, this could take a few.

And Your Name Is?

Chris Quintos

JACK, late teens to early 20s

The shy, quiet JACK, *a barrista, confesses details to his older sister about his crush on a customer named Carrie and the man he wishes he was.*

JACK   Carrie. Her name is Carrie. C-a-r-r-i-e. She comes in every day and she is...she's just really cute. I think I'm in love with her. Which is crazy, because I've never said more than five words to her. Mostly, "What can I get for you today?" And then calling her name when her drink is done. She works at the Forever 21 on Market Street.

I don't know how people do it. I have this coworker, Tim, he just flirts with everyone. I dunno, he's like twenty-one or twenty-two or something, so he's a little older than me. But like—he's got mad game. You know? Like, I feel like Beyoncé could walk in here tomorrow, and Tim would get her laughing in thirty seconds. It's like watching a magician. Like, where does he come up with this stuff, you know? It's hard enough for me to ask what people want to drink. And I'm supposed to do that. And then calling out names—that part is hard, too. I guess because I'm kind of quiet. Except for Carrie—if I'm working the register, I don't even ask. "Tall Iced Chai with Soy for Carrie." I don't know. Like sometimes, I'll be floating around in my mind while I'm making drinks, then when I have to call out a name, I do it quietly. And then I know it's like—I HAVE to do it again. But I'm like—ugh—why didn't I say it loudly to begin with? If I just said it with a little confidence, I wouldn't have to repeat myself.

Tim never repeats himself. Well, unless maybe the customer isn't paying attention. And then he'll add a joke, like, "Slightly less warm unclaimed Americano for Tom." God, Tim is so cool. Like, why am I so timid. Like I know this Half-Caff Latte is for Matt—I've made it for him for like four months, most mornings. So, why can't I just say that, "Half-Caff Latte for Matt. Half-Caff Latte for Matt." Twice, with confidence. And like, Matt—that's like a normal name. Don't even get me started on the hard names. Like—are q's supposed to sound like c's or k's? So hard to keep track. And like—apparently there's more than one way to say and spell every name you thought you knew. Like, not "Matt"—because "Matt" is pretty self-explanatory—but like "Sonia." Some people are like super specific, like it's "So-ni-ah" or like "Son-ya."

I don't know. Or like if I spell something with a y instead of an ie, that like could ruin someone's day. You know? It could end up on their Instagram as an FML. And I don't want that.

I make sure to spell Carrie's name right every time. I get upset when other people don't. Sometimes they spell it, K-e-r-r-y or C-a-r-e-y. But like, Tim? He could spell her name with a Z and she'd still laugh at his jokes. I just know she would.

Steak vs. Bologna

Hannah Gansen

DENNIS, 40

DENNIS *works in real estate, and is separated from his wife. He had moved from New York City to San Diego for about four months, but is now back in NYC for a bit to do some work for a client. In this scene, he in a whiskey bar, catching up with his friend Chad, 34, who is also in real estate.*

DENNIS   Everybody likes steak, right? Steak is great. But steak every day? Go home every night…and you're having steak… After a while, you want something different. Anything! Hell, even bologna sounds good. And eh, why not? You're drunk, you want something different, and shit…the bologna…it's right there!! And nobody needs to know. If your friends find out, you just say, "Hey, I was drunk!"

Sure, it's not something to be proud of…there's a reason you order steak in a public restaurant and not bologna. But bologna, she's got a pretty face, right?…In dim lighting?…right?

You're okay with bologna, 'cause bologna KNOWS it's bologna…but look out for spam. Spam THINKS it's something special, all held up in a can…And when you open that can, you can't just have a little spam. Spam will keep shoving her open can in your face, demanding you, "Eat me!

Eat all of me! You opened me! If you didn't want to eat all of me, then why did you open me in the first place?" And spams leave their empty cans behind so that steak will eventually find out. Then steak leaves you, and only then you realize that steak is rare AND well done.

So, best to just settle for a burger.

Potato salad on the side, though, instead of the fries.

Beef—It's What's for Dinner

Kate Ruppert

BEN, 34

BEN *is breaking the fourth wall and just talking to no one in particular at the audience.—and with no particular motive. It could be because of the color red that reminded him of ketchup, or the Pharell hat that reminded him of the hipster waiter—who knows?…An aside, independent of the situation…*

There are three thoughts going through BEN*'s mind:*
1.) I fucking hate having to cut my burger in half. The same goes for my any and all of sannys, but you didn't ask about sannys, so that's neither here nor there.
2.) I feel like the servers and/or chefs don't really believe me when I say "rare" and they try to second-guess me by serving a medium damn hamburger.
C.) At this particular restaurant, and two times in a row, this chef—who was a friend of mine-ish and had chosen a particular bun for his burger and a sauce for its bun and the perfect onion slices for the perfectly manageably sized patty and all the stars having aligned—delivered to me a basically raw humble masterpiece because he understood me on a level that was clear…suddenly and somehow defining that burger as #1 in my up-until-that-very-moment unconscious ranking of burgers in my lifetime.

BEN   They say it always happens when you least expect it. You find the one. And they're right; that's exactly how it happened.

If you think about it, we unknowingly rank and rate everything. We look for the best without actually making a pros-and-cons list, or pitting one against the other—it's just an ongoing process of natural sussing out until we've arrived at a completely unconscious conclusion. Happens every day. Happened to me; I found the best one without looking for it, and without even knowing I wanted to find it, honestly. But when I saw it, I knew.

Okay, so backstory. I always order beef. I crave it pretty much all and every day. Allegedly, it's because I have type O blood, and our people need red meat more than the others, but my craving is carnal. I cannot get enough. Usually, I'll get a filet, but I wouldn't do that at lunch, because I'm not an asshole. Anyway, I went to this place for an early lunch on a random Wednesday in a complete downpour with two people from the same walk of life who happened to be in town for different reasons. I ordered the burger. I actually almost lost my shit because it was listed last on the tiny menu, and once I read through the other seven items, I didn't think they'd even *have* a burger. But, okay, so it was there, and I ordered it from our uber hipster waiter—who wasn't really a hipster, he was too nice, but he *was* left-handed, which is another thing, I guess, that I unconsciously tabulate....I get my shit "cooked" rare. And not just rare, but in the words of my friend Matt Adams, "just walk it through a warm room." I'll go into the burger itself in just a minute.

But first, cut to last night. In the middle of the day, something came up, and I needed to stay late at the office. And not because I had shit to do, but because I had to wait for someone else to take care of *his* shit, so I had to kill time. In the words of every successful airport business plan, the easiest way to kill time is to go to a bar. I needed my bar to serve food, though, and all I could think about was that burger, so I bribed a coworker with dinner. And, this was the catch: The chef at this particular restaurant is the brother of a girl I've slept with, and, maybe, am still dabbling in. He knows me, but not really, and as much as I wanted that fucking burger, I didn't want him knowing I was there. Again. I told my coworker friend that it had to be a straight-up recon mission, like, Navy SEAL shit. We get in, and we get out. He cannot see me. I should mention the restaurant seats, maybe, forty people. Anyway, so we went. It was, easily, my seventh hamburger in as many days. And, I have to admit, that, when I ordered it, I ordered it as if the server had never had someone order a rare burger before. I wasn't rude, but I kinda spoke slowly and raised my eyebrows, like, we're on the same page, right? I feel bad; she was hot. Anyway. The burger comes to the table for the second time in less than five days, and my heart sped up, because I knew what I was in for. I'd not just been looking forward to it for the past four hours, but I'd been thinking about it since I had it the week before—which I've never done with a burger, I should have known my brain was working on something huge. When the plate landed on the table, it hit me so fast, I almost didn't notice it: I realized I was engaged in a full-on hamburger-ranking contest that'd been going on for quite some time, and it all came to right here, right now, with this perfect hamburger, and immediately, this unconscious, natural sussing out flashed to the forefront of my mind like in a Jason Bourne movie where every moment of my life hurdles itself forward through the consciousness. Two thoughts beca—three thoughts—became clear: One: I hate having to cut my burger in half, which inevitably makes me feel like a pussy. I want to pick it up and consume the entire thing without worrying about getting it on my tie. Two: I guess I've constantly felt like the server and/or "chef" assumes I've misspoken, or like I don't know what I really want in life, when I ask them to make it as rare as health code will allow, and I'll be served a burger that is too cooked, and you can't unfire or unruin a piece of meat. Or C. And this was the catalyst for realizing ANY of these three things were even thoughts—the chef—no insult of air-quotes required—served me, for a second time in less than a week, a basically-raw beef patty in a seeming attempt to call my bluff. Well, challenge accepted, Genius, because, short of eating it out of a bowl with a spoon, that's exactly the way I want it. And that's when it all made sense. The burger was the size of one my dad used to throw on the grill, but it was definitely not something my dad would have taken *off* the grill. Bigger is not always better. This gem was more like oh-shit-I-can-just-pick-it-up-and-eat-it, but in an absolutely unattainable way for a civilian like myself. Like, it wasn't some backyard BBQ burger, it was a fucking *burger*—you could tell by looking at it. The onions were slight, but not passive, and since they were there, I figured the chef had a reason, so I ate the fucking onions. And the lettuce on the bun was, not only fancy lettuce, but it was hand-snapped to fit perfectly without going over the sides of the bun—which is a pet peeve I also came to realize I had. Speaking of the bun. It was toasted, but not hard, so I could bite the fuck into it without thinking to myself, "this bun is pretty toasted," instead of, "this hamburger is fucking insane." You know?, it was approachable. Ain't too many fourteen dollar burgers that are approachable, know what I mean? I could've had it on a date (with his sister or that hot server) and looked like a fucking champ, while still only needing one napkin—and it was a fucking cloth napkin, because it was also the classiest burger in this unconscious competition. I'm serious right now, even as I'm talking about it, I'm realizing even more shit that made it so perfect. And "made" in the past tense like I'll never have it again…it's like, an option all the time—do you know how happy that makes me? And, actually, you know what, I'm sorry, I can't even talk about this anymore. I'm gonna do just that. I've gotta go see about a burger.…

Cloud Nine

Leah Mann

GERRY, 60s-80s

GERRY *has just arrived in heaven. He's wearing his hospital gown. He pats down his hair and tries to make himself more presentable.*

GERRY [*Looking around in awe.*] Huh. Not too shabby. Fluffy clouds, blue sky, warm, breezy. And hey! No more pain.

[*Does a little jig.*]

Hot damn, look at that! No achy joints, no nausea, no needles in my arms! This heaven thing is pretty great. Course next to cancer, what isn't? Talk about a low bar. Holy guacamole, that's Pop Pop and Nana!

[*Beat.*]

I hope Mother's not up here. That would have taken some deathbed repenting on her part.

[*Beat.*]

Hey…I wonder if Evelyn is here. I've been dreaming about that piece of cherry pie since my voice dropped. Oooh mama, there she is. Ask and ye shall receive. No mere earthly delights for me. Evelyn! It's me! Gerry! Remember? Back from the old neighborhood. Wowza, don't you look great? I just got here,

new kid on the block so to speak. Maybe you can give me a
tour, I can't think of a better welcoming committee. God,
you're as gorgeous as I remember. Talk about an angel!

[*Beat.*]

God! Hello there, um, sir. Gerald Johnson here. Yes, sir. Didn't
mean to call you "sir." Just an expression. Thank you, I'm
delighted to be here. Yes, I will be more judicious summoning
you in the future.

[*Beat.*]

Big man himself. That's service! Gonna have to watch my
language. Evelyn, honey, tell me about you. I read your obit a
few years back. What a tragedy! You stay married to Bucky for
forty years?! And of course you had that heart attack. I'm
kidding around. I'm glad it was quick, though trust me—that's
the way to go.

[*Beat.*]

Me? I spent three years dying. Takes all the drama out of an
exit. I said good-bye to my loved ones a dozen times before I
finally did them the courtesy of kicking the bucket. The bills,
the suffering, the bedsores...it was all very undignified.

[*Beat.*]

Not like you. You're like a queen. So you just stand there
looking beautiful and glowing with kindness and listen, because
I'm gonna lay it out for you.

[*Beat.*]

Evelyn—I love you. I've loved you since the day I set eyes on you. I've been dreaming about you for years and now you're here in the flesh and—well, now you're here. Let me woo you. Let me shower you with the affection you deserve. I want to kiss every inch of you, worship every hair on your head, breathe every word you speak into my lungs to hold onto you forever. And I mean forever. This is it. This is eternity and I want it with you.

[*Beat.*]

I know you chose Bucky all those years ago and I respect that. I never understood it, the guy's a chump and he never did treat you right, but that isn't my business. We got a second chance and I'm not gonna pass it up. Don't make the same mistake twice.

[*Beat.*]

Don't say no. I'm not some pimply kid stealing cigarettes to impress you anymore—I'm a man who's ready to fulfill you. I spent day after day, month after month, year after year with a good woman who never had my heart. I did my best to do right by her, but I have lived a shadow life. You, Evelyn, are my light, my vibrancy. You make my heart pound and my nerves ring out like delicately plucked lute strings. Let my death be the joyride my life never was. Ask me anything and I'll shoot straight with you. My soul is yours, open for you to read. Let me love you. Let me lavish myself upon you. Ask the moon of me, and I'll climb up from this cloud and drag it into heaven for you. Evelyn, you put me on cloud nine. What do you want? What is your greatest desire?

[*Beat.*]

bullets. I would be nearly panting as I dashed out the door with my sights set on the rendezvous point. My mom was usually shouting after me about some bullshit regarding spelling homework and I would shriek back in my squeaky voice, "MOM! I gotta go now! The enemy is approaching!!" She usually let me go without further protest and eventually she even let me have a BB gun, which immediately became my prized possession. "Hey, the kid seems to be obsessed with war games, I think a real gun is in order." She was a good woman my mother. She really understood me.

So this particular trip to the Boundary Waters had me pissing myself with excitement. The pretend jungle warfare was going to be so epic! Pat and I spent afternoons before the trip plotting on maps and crafting combat strategies. When we arrived at the campsite, four of Pat's uncles were standing around the fire drinking beer and comparing who could crush their cans with more brute force. There was quite the alpha male hierarchy going on and the head dog was Pat's oldest uncle named Carl. Carl was busy peacocking around the campsite, his magnificent beer gut glistening with a sheen of bug spray and sweat swelling over his belt. He loved barking orders at his younger brothers and delighted in calling them names like "numb nuts" and "dick bag." I decided to steer clear of Big Carl, and quietly went about unpacking all of the sweet supplies and weaponry I had brought along. I'm pretty sure I didn't bring a toothbrush, but by God I had a pretend snare trap made out of string and duct tape, among other essentials. In the center of the spread, I carefully laid out my shiny BB gun and stood back to admire my lot. Carl, who had been orchestrating an elaborate plan for roasting hot dogs, honed in on me then and lumbered over to inspect my stuff. He snorted and sneered as he called his brothers over, "Check this kid out! He's gonna protect us all from the big bad wolf!" Had I known better expletives back then I would have told him to "fuck off," but instead I offered a stern "shut up." It seemed to do the trick for the moment.

I strapped my BB gun over my shoulder to help elevate my standing in the pack of sweaty hounds and tried to broaden my shoulders as I came up to stand at the fire. Carl was cooking something in a cast-iron skillet, and he shoved it in front of me and Pat while trying to stifle a cross between a soggy belch and a belly laugh and he says, "You guys ever eaten a horse cock before?" The uncles nearly fell to pieces howling at Carl's hilarity. "Come on, you guys are tough, you gotta take a bite of this horse cock!" Okay, looking back, I clearly know that the member in the fry pan was some type of kielbasa, but at the time, it was all pretty upsetting. Pat and I exchanged nervous looks and his dad calling us over to the other side of the campsite saved us. He had set up some targets for us to shoot at. Now we're talking. So I set up shop behind the line he had marked off, and Pat and I took turns aiming at the target and pretending that we were avoiding enemy fire. All of a sudden we hear a squeal followed by the greatest string of swear words my eight-year-old ears had ever heard: "What the motherfucker, son of a bitch, whore's mother, ballsucker, shit, ass shit, fuck me, GODDAMMIT!" The realization, filled with both fear and victory, washed over me in slow motion. Big Carl had wandered off to take a piss and, in his inebriated wisdom, had decided to take care of business by the tree behind our target. My beautiful prized stallion of a BB gun had landed a bullet right in Big Carl's upper ass cheek—really more of his lower back—but with his bacony build, it was hard to tell.

Pat and I slowly backed away and strolled triumphantly back to the fire. "Who's the horse cock now?" Pat whispered under his breath as we plopped down and each took a bite of the kielbasa.

Camping at its finest.

Now, you ready to go on this Scout's adventure son? Grab your rucksack and let's tear this experience up.

Radio Silence

Kathy S Yamamoto

DJ GLAZED, 40-plus

DJ GLAZED *is an aspiring prime-time radio DJ who's stuck in the early-morning hours on a station in Benicia, CA. Though he's come short on his dream, he hasn't given up, and might've just found the key to his future.*

DJ GLAZED   Good evening, it is 3:23 on this beautiful Tuesday morning, and boy is it early. Yes, it is so early, but not too early for some smooth sounds on the radio. You're listening to *The Early Bird Gets the Love Song* here on Coast 101.8 FM. It's been another slow and steady morning for us over here at the station, and it looks like everyone in the Benicia area would rather sleep in than find love, but not to worry Benicia we at 101.8 FM, we are willing to wait for you to find love.

I guess this Tuesday will be another early morning dedicated to the love of my life: Jeanette Glazer, my mother. Jeanette, thank you so much for everything you do. For each of the thirty-eight—almost thirty-nine—years of my life. You are my light—my moon every night when you drive me to work, and every morning you are my sun, when you tuck me back in—

Oh, I'm getting word from my producer that we found a letter hidden under the ad tapes from the nineties in the vault. Wow, what a treat. Sorry, Mother, we will continue this later, perhaps in the car ride home!

[*Reads from an old letter.*]

   "December 23, 1986"

Wow, what a long time ago. If you wrote this letter, and you're listening, please feel free to call in. We'd love to hear from you and hear how your love life has changed over the past few decades. Let's continue.

   "Dear Craig,"

Aw, this is so sad. Craig Romanoff was the DJ in the 1980s here at the station, and he was going to move up to the 3:00 to 8:00 a.m. spot right before he died. Rest in peace, Craig.

[*Continues reading.*]

   "Dear Craig,

   I'm in love with a girl who doesn't know I exist. She is the most beautiful girl in the world. But not only is she beautiful, she is smart and kind and creative."

Wow, that is so sweet.

   "You told me yesterday I should talk to her, and I finally worked up the courage to talk to her, and I was confident in myself. After all, I am an incredibly attractive man."

Yes, confidence is often the key.

   "Unfortunately, this did not work out well. I'll spare you the details but it ended up incredibly humiliating for me. And I will seek revenge."

Oh no, this definitely took a turn for the worse.

> "I will kill you, Craig. I will take your eyeballs out and
> spread them over your kneecaps. I will kick your head
> around the field like a soccer ball."

Oh my God.

Wow. This is grotesque. And it keeps going. Well, to any
policemen on duty—I know there has to be some policemen on
duty—I urge you to come to the station and check out what
appears to be evidence of a heinous crime.

It looks like our mysterious scorned lover took his anger out on
an unsuspecting radio host. I guess I'll play "Cheek to Cheek"
by Frank Sinatra, for you, dear writer. I hope that justice finds
you, and that you don't find your way to the station to murder
me too. I do hope that you did get your girl in the end, and I
know that love will prevail for you, as it will for me, because
that's what Mother says.

In the meantime, Mother, if you want to pick me up a little
earlier, I would much appreciate it.

Death Party

Leah Mann

HAROLD, elderly

HAROLD, *elderly, ailing, in a wheelchair is dressed to the nines at a garden party.*

HAROLD   Welcome, so glad you could make it. You flatter, I look like crap, you old dog you. Canapé? Champagne? Please, help yourself. We're here to celebrate and don't tell me I'm not worth celebrating. It's been years, hasn't it? Just six months? I'll take your word for it.

[*Beat.*]

Can you remind me of your name again—George? My brother?

[*Beat.*]

Of course, little brother George!

[*Beat.*]

Have I told you what I've been up to? Let's see, I flipped a few houses for an incredible profit, sold one to a Saudi prince. I know there are dozens of them and one of them is living in my house. Nice guy, nice guy.

[*Beat.*]

Get me a refill, will ya? Damned wheelchair, can't do anything. There's a good man. Sure, my arms work, but wheeling myself around is a pain in the ass and I got people who do it for me. That's living, am I right? For now at least. Ha! Let's be honest, for today at least. Let the countdown begin!

[*Beat.*]

What was I saying? Damn brain can't hold three thoughts in my head. Can still hold a drink, though. Is that cake? Where's the cake? I want my cake. It's got my face on it. Did you see that? Pretty impressive, huh? You ever have a cake with your face on it?

[*Beat.*]

Where did you come from again? New Mexico? Where is that? And you came all this way for me... You must really care about me.

[*Beat.*]

I'm so glad you made it. It'll probably be the last time, which is the whole point. Better to have a party where you get to see me than a funeral where everyone's sad and I'm already gone. Where's the fun in that? I want to see my friends before I go and it's any day now, really truly. Look at me—I'm falling apart. Dead to rights. Sometimes I wake up with bits of me—what's that word? You know—those things on cupcakes or ice cream? The little crunchy things?—Sprinkles, yes! I wake up with bits of me sprinkled around the blankets. Not a pretty picture, but that's death. What about you? Any plans to kick the bucket soon? You're what, eighty-five at least?

[*Beat.*]

Only seventy-one? Huh.

[*Beat.*]

Is that my grandson over there? Damn kids look different every time I see them with the beards and hair and everything. That's your grandson? Don't I have one? Couldn't make it? College my ass, that layabout is studying some nonsense like philosophy. Where's the living in that? What's yours studying? Medicine? Well la-di-dah for you.

[*Beat.*]

We've been brothers for a long time, haven't we?

[*Beat.*]

Seventy-one years? Is that right? You count all the years?

[*Beat.*]

Well you tried to steal my daughter from me and we didn't speak for a while. I don't remember much but I never forget a grudge! HA!

[*Beat.*]

Don't go squirming away—You said you helped her when I kicked her out for dating that delinquent and I say you went against my authority as a father and your older brother and harbored a fugitive. It's your damn fault she married the guy. Bah, love. Ridiculous. You think I loved my wife?

[*Beat.*]

Of course I miss her. I think about her every day. Sometimes
I'm sitting at home with the paper and I ask her to bring me a
sandwich before looking around and remembering she's gone.

[*Beat.*]

Will you miss me when I'm gone? I worry sometimes that
people won't miss me. You're my brother, you have to miss me,
right? We're all that's left these days. I got more friends in the
obits. I don't know half these damn people eating my cake.

[*Beat.*]

I guess they know me, though.

[*Beat.*]

But you and me, we've been through a lot. Even though you're
a kidnapper and backstabber, you're still my little brother and
that means something to me. We survived mom and pop, didn't
we? I fought in that war. The second one, I think. When I got
back, who met me at the docks? You. Who bought you your
first hooker? Me. That's bonding. That's family. Who else is
there for you all the way through?

[*Beat.*]

And you're here now, still seeing me all the way through.

[*Tearing up.*]

I love you. I want you to know that. When you go back to
Mexico, you don't forget that your big brother loves you and
forgives you. Don't be too hard on yourself. We all make
mistakes in our life. So what if you made more than most?

[*Beat.*]

Where's my damn cake?

[*Beat.*]

Will ya go get me some cake already? I hope it's better than last year's cake. That was a dud. I don't remember much, but I remember that. Boy did I give it to the bakery when I tasted that cake. Who gives a dying man a bad cake at his good-bye party?

[*Beat.*]

How many of these do they think a person has? Two, three at most.

[*Beat.*]

What was your name again?

Gee Golly Gosh

Rachel Raines

JOSHUA, 25 to 35

JOSHUA is discussing a recent visit from his in-laws with a close male friend in his home, probably the kitchen. JOSHUA is more bemused that annoyed by his father-in-law. He admires the man but feels that they cannot understand one another, even though they get along well enough.

JOSHUA He actually wants me to say things like "gee golly gosh" when I am around him. That's how my father-in-law sees me. I find it pretty amusing. Like, "Gee golly gosh, Mr. Andrews, I fucked your daughter from behind so hard last night she came twice!" He seems to think we live like that family from *Leave It to Beaver* when he's not around.

I don't know why he got that in his head. Yeah, I'm a nice guy, but I never put on a sweater-vest or talked about having a low tolerance for dairy. We see each other a few times a year and it's nice, everyone is nice but nothing fits into a frame, you know? Like, yesterday I found him cleaning out our gutters. And he was actually wearing these thick gardening gloves to do it. We do not own gardening gloves. My wife and I are into some kinky stuff, but we've never owned gardening gloves in our life. He might have found the handcuffs and fireman's hat in the back of the closet but not *gardening gloves*. I mentioned it to

Sarah, and she said he brought them along. He packed his own gloves, in anticipation of doing yard work. According to her, he wants us to mow the damn lawn together tomorrow. It's bonding to him, she says. I told her he would be pretty surprised at the kind of "bonding" we generally do in the yard. (Just once, late at night, pretty drunk. It was fun.) She threw a dishtowel at me. (Funny, before I got married I wouldn't have known what a "dishtowel" was. A towel is a towel. But I've heard my father-in-law say it so many times cleaning up our kitchen, I just know it now.)

The Andrews's have got a great marriage and I know they're happy their daughter does, too—I just don't think they know their daughter all that *well*. We're going to the beach tomorrow and I'll be damned if we're not having sex in the woods. We are so sneaking off and getting in a quickie. Sarah likes it when her folks are just out of range, like she's in high school again. And then we'll come back hair smoothed, all smiles and eat her father's potato salad and shredded chicken. The man is a picnic wizard. He should do it for money.

After the gutters were cleared, he actually asked me if I wanted to "throw the ball around." I was *this close*—really, this close—thank god I don't have a loose tongue (Sarah would find a dirty joke in that phrase, I know it—something about oral sex)—but no, really, *this close* to asking him which balls he'd like to be tossing about. Mine aren't detachable. Sarah would have killed me.

We did it. Tossed around the ball. For like twenty minutes before I was able to say I needed a shower. I found him reading the paper after, on the back porch with a mug of tea. The man could be a *Saturday Evening Post* model.

The thing is, for the rest of my life I'll keep this up. I'll play along because, hey, it's family and he's a nice guy. I've got no complaints. But next time *we* visit *them*, there will be some serious ball tossing, and it's happening on their bed.

Chip

Steve Brian

This is a monologue from the play, *Off the Old Block*, written by Steve Brian.

CHIP, 21

CHIP *has been taken in for questioning about the theft of some supplies from the paper-distributing company he works for and misunderstands the interrogation, thinking that he is about to be murdered.*

NOTE: Feel free to change the character's age to match your own.

CHIP   Please don't kill me, I just turned twenty-one years old, and I haven't even had a threesome...well, with two girls, anyway.

[*Beat.*]

If I am gonna die, though, on the real, I need to confess that I cheated on my SATs...and I didn't actually kiss Kelly in the playhouse back in first grade. Can you please tell Cody? And one time, when I was coming home from a party at like, 3:00 a.m., I started talking to this tranny hooker and I went home with her and started screaming because I thought she stole my wallet, but really, I had just left it at home in the first place in the front left pocket of this vest that I really don't ever wear, but I thought she stole it so I started screaming and kicked a

door and the cops came and I got arrested and went to the
drunk tank and all I was wearing was board shorts and a
wife-beater and my BFF Jay had drawn a tribal tattoo on my
arm with a sharpie for the club—cuz chicks dig tattoos—and
this really big guy in the drunk tank who kinda looked like
Nick Nolte, but before he was crazy and still actually kinda
handsome—anyway, this guy told me that I could blow him or
he'd rape me...so I blew him...and I liked it.

I think I might be gay?

Actually, I don't think I am, I know I am and it feels really good
to just say that, out loud. I don't even want to have a threesome
with two girls. I just want to find a gay boyfriend that looks just
like me and settle down and have a cat or something...or a
dog, but a big one, 'cause the little ones freak me out and then
I'd have to get one of those Bergan pet carriers for when I
travel...or I could adopt. Can gay guys adopt? I've always
wanted to get married. Am I gonna be able to get married?
Can't gay people get married in, like, I think Vermont or
something? I dunno. I guess I see why these gay people want
equal rights with marriage, 'cause when I was still straight just,
like, a minute ago, if you woulda asked me about this topic, I
probably woulda said something like, "Gays don't belong in the
marriage circle. Marriage is for men and women. That's what it
says in the Bible." But if you really think about it, the Bible is
full of contradictions; I mean, you really think Mary was a
virgin? Me, either. I bet Joseph played just the tip, like, one
time, and then Mary was like, "Joey, I want to be able to wear
white on my wedding," and Joseph was like, "C'mon, babe, let
me just put the tip of it in," and she was like, "Okay, Joey, but
just this once." But, like, some of that premature ejaculation
shit musta come out and that musta been how Mary got

pregnant, but then the wise men were like, "How'd you get pregnant?" and Mary was like, "I don't know, it's a miracle," and they all believed her. I mean, at that point in history, they didn't really know how babies came, did they? But since they didn't know that, how could they have known that God wants us to be one man, one woman, y'know? I mean maybe he really meant every relationship should be half masculine, half feminine in order for it to be successful, and I know plenty of gay dudes that are feminine or butch lesbos that are real masculine, so they just make up the right ratio in the 50/50 feminine-masculine equation. I mean I guess it could also be like 60/40 or 20/80, just so long as you have a good ratio.

[*Silence, as his epiphany settles in.*]

So, are you gonna kill me because I'm gay now? I mean, if you are gonna kill me, can you please call me Chip?

I Didn't Kill My Wife

Jessica Glassberg

JEFFREY WALSH, 50s

JEFFREY WALSH, *crestfallen, sits in a chair talking to a police officer.*

JEFFREY   My name…um, for the record, is Jeffrey Walsh. I am here about the passing of my wife…

[*Choked up.*]

Please don't make me say "potential murder." I just…She was my soul.

[*Taking a deep breath.*]

For the…potential murder of my wife, Clara Walsh, on Wednesday, January the 18th.

[JEFFREY *sips his water.*]

As I told the other officer, at the time of my wife's death, I was out with her sister, Gwen. We were looking for a birthday present for Clara.

[*Choked up.*]

Our dear, dear, Clara. Clara's birthday is February 4th, and we were looking for a present on January 18th. We had plenty of time to find something we loved. That we knew Clara would love. So, Gwen and I went downtown together to shop. I picked her up at noon. Well, I got there at twelve-oh-three, and man did she rag on me for being late.

[*He laughs.*]

Then, she kept changing the radio station. I don't think we heard one complete song the whole way into the city. Must be a family thing. Clara does…did that.

Anyway, then we shopped…

[JEFFREY *takes another sip of water.*]

Oh yes. Before we went shopping, Gwen and I did have lunch at Pagliacci's. I had the spaghetti Bolognese and Gwen had the chicken Marsala.

[*He says, with a smile.*]

Actually, she ended up eating half of my spaghetti. Why don't people want what they already have? She always does that. Orders something and then wants what I'm enjoying.

[*Catching himself.*]

Not that we always do anything together. She's just my sister-in-law…well, was. I guess that title goes away now that my wife's gone.

[*Then…*]

G-d rest her soul.

[*Smiling.*]

It's funny; I've always known Gwen as my sister-in-law; now she's just Gwen. I mean, there's no law saying we can't still go out for pasta together. There isn't, right?

[*Beat.*]

Okay, good. Anyway, we had some pasta...a few laughs.

[JEFFREY *has another sip of water.*]

Um, yes, we did have a few glasses of wine. Well, we each had one. One each. One glass of wine for each of us.

[JEFFREY *takes another, longer sip.*]

What did we get? I told you the spaghetti Bol—Oh, what present did we get? We, ya see, we didn't end up getting the present that day.

[JEFFREY *takes a deep breath and goes to take another sip of water. The cup is empty.*]

We didn't find anything we really liked. That Clara would really like. We wanted something special...for Clara.

[*Wiping his brow.*]

Oh, the bracelet. The bracelet on my credit card statement? Yes, the bracelet. I know I said I didn't get her anything. And, the bracelet wasn't for Clara. For...Clara's birthday. It wasn't a present for Clara's birthday. It was more of a "just because," present.

[*Taking a breath.*]

Well, right now Gwen actually has it. It...so...she wanted it because, ya know, for the sentimental value. Because we bought it together. For Clara. But right, like I said, it was not Clara's birthday present.

[*Standing up.*]

Well, why the hell would I get Clara a birthday present if I knew by the time her birthday rolled around, she'd be dead!?!?

Healthy Living

Carla Cackowski

MIDDLE-AGED MAN, mid-40s to mid-50s

A MIDDLE-AGED MAN *approaches the check-in desk at a gym.*

MIDDLE-AGED MAN   Excuse me, Miss. Excuse me. Miss. Miss! Sorry to interrupt the podcast you're listening to—supposedly you're at work?—but that elliptical machine over there isn't working properly.

I know it's not working properly because I was just on it. And it didn't work. And so I wasn't able to exercise. Currently, at this moment in time, that elliptical machine is the definition of not working.

No need to glare at me. Not my fault your company's equipment isn't working.

Huh? No, I will not wait for a new machine. I want a new machine now. Let me give you a little tip here, Mam. That's right. I was trying to be polite with "Miss," but your attitude has graduated you to "Mam." I pay you guys money each month to work out when I want to work out. If I show up and can't work out because you guys can't keep up maintenance on the machines I help pay for, then what am I paying you for?

What is your problem? That look you're giving me. The way you're glaring at me, you're glaring at me like this is my fault. Oh, I know what you're thinking. That look in your eyes is crystal clear. You're thinking, "Maybe it is his fault. Maybe he's so fat he broke the machine. Or maybe he's too stupid to make it work properly." You're thinking, "Maybe the machine's not broken, maybe he's broken." That's what your glare is telling me right now.

What do you mean, it hasn't been working for a week? Wait. So it *has* been working? So, what you're saying is that sometimes it works, and sometimes it does not work. Oh, is that so? Then why isn't there a sign? On the machine. To say it isn't working. Sometimes. Working sometimes. I mean, how else are we supposed to know that it sometimes doesn't work if there's not a sign to tell us Only Sometimes Working?!

No. I will not wait for a new machine! I stood in the elliptical machine line for fifteen minutes this morning waiting for an elliptical machine so I could get in my thirty minutes of cardio on the damn elliptical machine and now you're telling me that because the elliptical machine that was working when the person before me was on it but now isn't working when I'm on it, that it only sometimes works, you're telling me I'm screwed and have to stand in line all over again?

Well, I call bullshit on you. You need to make my machine work. Or put up a sign. Or, or, OR I should get the next elliptical machine that opens up!

I will? Damn right I will. Okay, good. And until I do, I'm going to stand right here and glare at you. Because you deserve it.

[*Beat.*]

What is that podcast you're listening to? How can you listen to
that stuff? That guy sounds like an angry asshole.

Man Scout

Andy Goldenberg

RICHIE RANDALL, 30s to 50s

RICHIE, *an impassioned father, speaks up at the local Boy Scouts Chapter.*

RICHIE   YAWN! Someone wake me when this conversation gets interesting! This is the most boring meeting I have ever been a part of, and I'm an accountant! I don't know about the rest of you, but for the last twenty minutes, I've been sitting here wondering why I ever wanted my son to be a Boy Scout in the first place! What I've always really wanted was for my son to be a MAN Scout. I want him to get some real Scout badges for doing real things like us real men do. I don't mean like tying a knot or fighting a grizzly bear. I mean, a REAL MAN. We should be giving our kids badges like...Sitting on the couch with nothing to do for an ENTIRE DAY. That takes some skill, right Bob? Or going a full week without bathing. Or going a full month without doing laundry. Or spending your entire life having always gotten out of bathroom duty, like Steve over here. Would our boys be able to achieve those honors, or have we made sissies of them? We've inoculated them from diseases by not letting them eat off of the floor in five-second-rule fashion. We've withheld the joys of seeing naked women with our harsh Internet parental controls.

Gentlemen of Boy Scout Troop 365, we have mothered our boys for far too long, and it is time that we STOPPED! Let them get badges for realizing how to cheat the government out of their hard-earned money. Let 'em have a badge if they elude capture not only from an ex-wife, but an illegitimate child. One badge for each kid. Rack 'em up, right Troy?

Wouldn't it be great if we gave them a badge for pounding down drink after drink at the bar and NOT cheating on their spouse or NOT getting killed on the treacherous way back to their house in the hills? Rest in peace, Sammy. You were a man. A REAL man. And what you accomplished in your life was worth more than any merit badge for sustainability, landscape architecture, or Scouting Heritage. When can we dig into the refreshments that Paul brought, because I could sure use a lemon-lime Gatorade and orange slice right about now.

Brownies

Chris Quintos

SON, mid- to late 20s

A devoted SON *in his mid- to late 20s who doesn't usually share much about his dating life, until now. He speaks to his mom, who is in the hospital.*

SON   No, Mom. I got it. Trust me. I can handle making something for the church bake sale. Because I don't want you to have to worry about any of this kind of stuff!

Because your main job is to get rest and recover.

Because I didn't just have major surgery! I'll probably make brownies. Give me a little credit, Mom. I've cracked an egg into brownie mix before, believe me.

What do you mean, when? When I made brownies, that's when. Mom—I know you love me, and I know I'm your son, but you don't know EVERYTHING about me. You just don't! Like, like—well, you didn't know that I've made brownies before.

Yes. Yes, for Melissa.

What do you mean? Because brownies were like her favorite thing.

Mom. We made them a lot. She got cravings for them at crazy times. She even packed mix when we traveled! It was pretty cute. Oh—I think I even have this special brownie pan in my apartment that makes it so that every piece has edges.

Mix is just as good as from scratch. What do you mean, how do I know? Because, we did side-by-side taste tests. You just have to get the right mix and spruce it up a little.

Well, you can add mini chocolate chips, or peanut butter chips. With macadamia nuts, maybe? Then right when they come out, you sprinkle a little sea salt on top. WHY am I telling you this???

Yes, sea salt—because sweet plus salty is like everyone's favorite thing.

Yes. Of course I miss her.

Look, Mom, I miss her and I don't want to talk about it!

I didn't mean to snap. Just get some rest and don't worry about the bake sale. My brownies will be great. Maybe I'll even make an extra batch for you.

Yes, they'll have sea salt on top. Now get some rest. Single son's orders.

L'aissez Fritte

Brandon Econ

ALAN GREGORY, 29

ALAN *is an effete intellectual who thinks he knows how the world works because he read about it in a textbook. Justified in his beliefs, but thoroughly unvalidated or self-aware, Alan makes it his mission to take offense at everything because he thinks being critical is the same as being smart. He's talking to a Cashier, Jennifer, at a McDonalds near a college campus.*

ALAN   I don't do this very often [*Looking at name tag.*], Jennifer. But, these fries, well I don't even know how you call these "fries." If a customer such as myself's first experience with your establishment is one in which the quote "America's Favorite Fries" are in complete disarray, what do you think are my chances for a return visit? Any thoughts?

I'd guessed as much. I haven't had service this bad since the Pinkerton's were called in to break up the strike on Carnegie Steel. I assume . . .

And look at this, a McNugget. It's as if you are attempting to derive some sort of aesthetic from Irish chickens and pit them against Americans, in what is clearly the most blatant exercise of xenophobia, I ASSUME, since the Alien and Sedition Acts were repealed. Why does everything need to have the family name anyway? It's as if "nugget" is some sort of pagan word derived from the root of some Luftwaffe word for "gas chamber," and adding "Mc" in some way rectifies the situation. Do you find comfort in working for a fascist company, Jennifer?

Oh, you don't think so? What do they call you at the barracks, McHitler Youth?

Fascinating. Well then, how do you justify weakening the dollar in a global market? Don't you find it morally reprehensible to devalue the cost of produce in the middle of a recession and place it on a dollar menu. It's as if you have nationalized every aspect of our agricultural system. Perhaps it is really some hyper altruistic cabal that finds it necessary to keep the dollar in a state of disrepair in order to pander to a downtrodden populace scratching for some sense of identity. I can tell with the utmost sincerity that I am indeed not lovin' it.

To be perfectly frank. I find it disturbing that your mascot is a clown? Not only do you debase the constituents in your own country, but you portray Irish men in a light that is racist and degrading. It's as if you feel the need to enforce some forgotten code of ethics and label the Irish as a white-faced, red-haired super race.

I'm not going to step aside, Jennifer. I have a right to be here, this is a free country. I will not stand idly by while you give me marching orders and force me out into the dead of winter. If you want my advice. I recommend you give me the same attention you would any other customer.

Unbelievable.

I won't stand for it. Now you can either be the basis for all asceticism in this world and turn a jaundiced eye towards my needs or you can make sure the fries are well done next time. The decision is entirely yours.

Married Rant

Lynn Trickey

A MAN, 30s

A MAN *talks to his buddy.*

A MAN Hey man, I was thinking—I don't know, I had this kind of crazy idea, and, stay with me on this, but I was thinking, maybe, you and Claire, maybe...don't get married?

Look, man, I try not to be that single friend who is all antimarriage, but...you're making it kinda hard on me.

I mean, you and Claire seem to be really happy, but ever since this whole engagement thing happened, all I hear from you is "Planning a wedding is so hard! And it's expensive, and it's tough to make decisions, and blah!"

Oh wait, shit, sorry, do you *have* to get married? Like right now?

Is she Catholic?
Or, is her family super conservative? Will they disown her if you guys continue to live in sin?

No? Oh, okay then don't get—

Wait, is this like a health insurance thing?
Or are you trying to get some tax breaks, or...?

Oh, okay, then don't get—

Is this a green card thing?
Or some political statement I'm not understanding?

Oh, okay, then don't get—

[*Ticking off reasons on his hands.*]

Are you moving to the Bible Belt?
Converting to Islam?
Looking to get in on that sister-wife thing and wanna make it legal?

Is a grandparent dying?
Are either of you suffering from a terminal illness?
Do you have to be married in order to qualify for some sort of inheritance a la the 1999 Chris O'Donnell/Renée Zellweger film *The Bachelor*?

No?

[*He gets faster and more erratic as he ticks off ideas.*]

Are you adopting a child and you need to become more desirable candidates? Looking to gain custody of children from a previous marriage to spite your ex? Do you already have some bastard children who are just now getting to the age that they can ask, "Why are my mommy and daddy not married?" And they're really hounding you?

Do you already have some bastard dogs who are just now getting to the age that they learned human speech and they're all "why are my mommy and daddy not married?" And they're really *HOUNDING* you? (That was a dog pun).

Is this a scam to register for a bunch of stand mixers on your gift registry and then resell them on eBay?

Do you have to break some sort of gypsy curse?

Or are you looking for a really good excuse to get out of the priesthood?

Does she just have a bunch of flowers and a really great-fitting white dress lying around and you're all, "WHAT THE HAY!"

Is one of you really old and wealthy and the other Anna Nicole Smith?

OH, IS ONE OF YOU GEORGE CLOONEY? BECAUSE THAT MAKES SENSE IF SHE IS ACTUALLY GEORGE CLOONEY STOP WHAT YOU'RE DOING, GO DOWN TO THE COURTHOUSE, AND LOCK THAT DOWN!

[*Shouting now.*]

BUT IF YOU'RE JUST HAVING A HARD TIME WITH THE IDEA OF GETTING ALL THE PEOPLE WHO LOVE YOU IN ONE ROOM TO CELEBRATE YOUR CHOICE TO SPEND YOUR LIFE WITH YOUR ROMANTIC PARTNER, IF THAT'S TOO MUCH FOR YOU TO HANDLE? THEN MAYBE DON'T GET MARRIED!

[*He takes a deep breath, composes himself.*]

Yeah, but like I said, happy to be the best man and all. Mazel tov.

Baby Daddy in Prison

Alessandra Rizzotti

SEMAJ, 19 to 25

SEMAJ *sits in his prison cell after a visit from his girlfriend. He is talking to his cellmate.*

SEMAJ   Man, why do women gotta be buggin'? My girl is gettin' on me for not being able to get out o' lockdown for my baby's first birthday. She's all in my lunch tryin' to figure out what I do here all day. You know we don't do nothin'. She want me to bake a cake or somethin'? Blow up balloons? I'm about to jump the couch!

[*He sighs, plopping down on the bed, staring at the ceiling.*]

Her mama sayin' we shouldn't have this baby, but I know we's able to do it. Shit, I don' never knew my dad. I'm not perfect or nothin', but I have a lot o' love to give. At least I gonna get to know this baby. I would give up my Sega Game Gear for a new baby carriage, ya know? Wheat bread instead of Cheetos, right? No more Red Bull. Just milk, right? They say you have to be healthy and shit when you gonna be raisin' babies, so I gon' have to stop hittin' up 7-Eleven for dem frozen dinners and breakfast burritos. I'll prob'ly sell my skateboard so I can get dem diapers too.

Life's about payin' the bills, and when you don't, you go put yo'self out on the street. I ain't here because I wanted to. I was just survivin'. My brotha said I could go do a deal, and then the po-po showed in the hood right when I got there. Shiiit. I'll be out when the baby is like one and a half, though. At least it's not ten years, right?

Man, what are you in here for? Ohhhhh duuude, I forgot. You prob'ly won't see your kids ever again...woah...I didn't mean to offend you or nothin' in sayin' that, but truth's the truth.

[*He pauses and looks over his shoulder.*]

Thanks for not beatin' my ass when I said that.

When you have babies and shit, you gotta be calm and not get angry or nothin', just like you right now starin' at the ceilin' like it's some kinda blingin' Jesus on a cross. My baby mama was telling me just now how she saw a g-ma yell at her grandkid for not wearing socks and it's like, babies don't put on socks by themselves, so why are you yellin'? We would never yell at our baby. No way. We is goin' to talk like she is loved. We's gonna tell her she is a princess and that she gonna grow up to be a hair stylist, or whatevah. I don't know math or nothin', but I would git her in school so she could learn it. My boys, we deal with numbers in our business, but I wouldn't want the baby mixed in that. D.A.R.E. to keep babies off the streets, ya know? Ha-ha.

I should learn from my mistakes, but I don't know how else to make money at this point. What do you do after you get out of here? Oh wait, you probl'y don't care.

My baby mama is in school at the city college. She's gonna be a nurse. She's smarter than me. Well, obviously. She ain't here.

Ha. Oh lord, please help me get out of here so I can start ovah. It's harder to be a person than to create one, ya know what I mean?

Hey—you listenin'?

[*He turns back to his cellmate.*]

Yo, you always be dissin' me, fallin' asleep when I'm talkin'. You wack.

Folks in Town

Leah Mann

KEVIN, early 20s

KEVIN, *a scruffy stoner in his early 20s, has just picked up his parents at the airport. The inside of his car, a 1995 Honda Accord, is dingy and littered with trash.*

KEVIN   Mom, Dad! Hi! How was your flight?

Yeah, give me a sec, I'll get your bags...let me just pop the trunk. Oh shit—I mean, shoot, sorry—I forgot to clear that stuff out of the backseat, just throw it on the floor. Yes, even the burrito, it's okay, I'm done with it. Everyone buckled in? Where's your hotel? Oh, you want to see my place first? Of course, that's fine! I thought you'd be tired. My roommates will be thrilled to meet you, in fact let me text real quick to let them know we're on the way. No, not text, because I'm driving. I'll give Georgie a call using my very safe and legal bluetooth.

[*Beat.*]

Georgie, hey brother, wanted to give you a heads up that my PARENTS and I are gonna be at the apartment in twenty minutes not that it means you should clean or do anything before we arrive, but just a polite notice of our imminent arrival.

[*Beat.*]

Mom, stop touching my hair—Let me hang up the phone!—
I like it like this. My beard, too. Beards are very hip these
days, I promise, the ladies love it. Girlfriend? Oh, that's not
what I meant. I mean, I date, but no one special. It's tough
out there, you know? To find someone you're on the same
page with who's interesting and fun but not demanding and
I don't have to go out of my way for too much, plus the
whole attraction thing...you can't ignore that, shallow or
not. I don't want to settle and I think the worst thing is to
lead a girl on.

[*Beat.*]

It's a matter of respect and honesty more than anything else.

[*Beat.*]

I'm trying to focus on work right now, build a stable life for
myself like you two taught me. Work is going great, totally.
I'm killing it. They aren't promoting anyone or giving anyone
raises because of the economy, you know double-dip and all
that, we're still recovering, but they totally value me. I'm great
with the customers, and I'm on the management track because
my computer and math skills are top-notch. Not calculus or
anything, but I'm great at the arithmetic for balancing out the
register at night and keeping inventory. You know—like how
many ketchup packets or buns we have in stock, that sort of
thing. I have you to thank for that, Dad. Denying me an
allowance as a kid made me very fiscally responsible—I never
lose a penny.

[*Beat.*]

There's change in the seat back there? That's not lost, that's for parking meters. Always be prepared! Yes, that is why I have condoms under that seat, thank you for noticing, Mom.

[*He pulls a sharp turn and changes route.*]

I also have an emergency kit in the trunk like a good Boy Scout. Don't look so surprised. I'm very adult now. I mean, fuck—sorry—I've been on my own for seven years now. I do my laundry and everything. Well, I drop it off at the Laundromat—which is a good deal and puts money back into the neighborhood. I consider it my civic duty to stimulate the local economy.

[*Beat.*]

You don't look impressed. You disapprove? You think real men do their own laundry instead of relying on hired help? Whatever, I don't need your approval, it'd be nice, I'd take it...I'm not being childish! You do approve then?

[*Beat.*]

You don't. My potential? Again with my potential? Oh look, we're here! Oops, did I go to your hotel? My bad. I must have been on automatic, you know how that goes, when your hands do the driving. As long as we're already here...let me just pop the trunk.

Morning After

Jeff Passino

KEITH, 30s

KEITH*'s bed, in his very small studio apartment.*

KEITH   Hey. Psst. Hey, Jenny. Are you awake? Ah that's okay, I guess you're not an early riser like me, huh? Ha-ha. Yeah, I'm a bit of a morning person. Admittedly not usually THIS much of a morning person, 6:00 a.m. is pretty early. I can't sleep, though. I just want to stay up and watch you sleep. Whoa, that sounded creepy coming out of my mouth. You're still asleep I hope, yeah? Ha-ha. Wait, are you? Okay, good. Yeah, you will find I do that a lot. So much stuff seems like a good idea to say in my head and then it comes out and blaaahhh, oh no what have I said. Ha-ha. That's why if you ever hear anyone around the office say that I'm a racist, it's...that was a big misunderstanding and...I'm a big believer in equality for everyone. Except for women, obviously. Ha-ha, no, obviously a joke. And a clear example of what I'm talking about. But that's my humor, too. You're probably like "What, the IT guy has a sense of humor?" Um yes, I do. People have even told me I should probably do stand-up. Well my parents have. My mom. And I'm like, "Mom, I don't think everyone is going to get it when I do an impression of Nana." Ha-ha-ha-ha-aaahhh. My mom is a big fan of the impression I do of my nana. You will probably like it, too. Though you won't have anything to compare it to, my nana died about five years ago.

What are you going to want for breakfast? I'll ask you again when you are actually awake, obviously, but just know I can make you anything you want. Whatever you are dreaming about right now in that pretty little head of yours, I'll make for you.

[*Whispering into her ear to get her to start dreaming about food.*] Blueberry pancakes. Hash browns. An egg, bacon, avocado breakfast sandwich. Raisin Bran. Oh yeah, anything at all you want I will make you. And then after breakfast if you want to just hang out with me for the rest of the day well, I guess that would be cool. Ha-ha. I did just get a couple new video games. An early Christmas present to myself. Oh gosh, I should... probably...I'm going to have to get you a Christmas present now, huh? Or, how long after people start dating is it before they get presents for each other usually? 'Cause it will be, let's see, Christmas is Wednesday and [*Counting on his fingers.*] Friday, Saturday, Sunday, Monday, Tuesday, Wed...well it will be like almost a week, I'm sure we can do a little something for each other. I mean I want to. You deserve it. It will be fun. I've never had a girlfriend on a holiday before. Yeah, this will be fun! Unless, you do celebrate Christmas, don't you? Of course you do, what are you a Jew? Joke there. Not that the Jewish faith is a joke, obviously. But you sure were in the celebrating spirit last night at the office party. I've never seen someone drink so much eggnog before. It must be good. I'm lactose intolerant, so I've never had it. I've never been extremely religious, so I've never had a huge reason to celebrate Christmas before, other than, you know, it's fun, I like the music. You know now that I think about it, if it weren't for

Christmas I wouldn't have ever known you even liked me. Eight years working in the same office and I could have sworn you were always calling me Heath instead of Keith. But after last night...I will be able to confidently tell our future children that Christmas miracles ARE real! Maybe I should thank Santa for bringing you here. Santa and, I guess, Scott, who I gather left without you or something? I'll have to finish getting that story from you. A lot of time when girls are crying I get very uncomfortable and have to count my breathing so I didn't really catch what you were saying. Oh...you're waking up. Hi. I've been watching you sleep.

Filthy Rich

Mark Harvey Levine

TAROT READER, late 30s to early 70s

A sleazy-looking street psychic, holding tarot cards and standing at a little fold-up table, accosts a stranger.

TAROT READER [*With a vague foreign accent.*] Here, come my friend. I give you a freebie. I read your tarot. I tell you your future. And this is freebie. This is free.

[*Turns over a card.*]

Look at the first card! Ahhh...I see already you're going to be rich! Yes, very rich, my friend. Filthy rich. Dirty, dirty, dirty, filthy rich. You will not be able to wash it off, that's how rich you'll be. Pigs rolling in their own slop will not be as soiled as the filthiness of your richitude.

[*Turns over a card.*]

And you will be rich many years, for I see a long life ahead of you. Long, long, LONG life. It will seem to go on forever! Friends, family will be dying all around you, and you—you will just keep living. And living. And then you turn around and you are living some more. You will live so long that you will beg and pray for the sweet release of merciful death—*that's* how long you'll live. And all this time? Filthy rich. Just nasty, squalidly... a *contamination* of riches. You will be Rich Out Loud.

[*Turns over a card.*]

Now this card here, this is the Six of Cups. It means you are going to have six cups. Not those plastic purple ones from Target, like you have now. No, my friend, these will be solid-gold goblets, because you're indecently rich and you actually think that's what wealthy people drink out of. They will be huge, heavy, gaudy things, with large jewels encrusted in them right where you would grab them, so that every time you pick them up you cut the hell out of your hands.

But you don't care because *that's how rich you are.* You can buy new skin, and you can buy new friends when they all leave you because you're doing things like buying immense gold goblets in the *worst* possible taste just to show them how very rancidly rich you are.

[*Turns over a card.*]

Which brings us to your love life. Because of your gigantic wealthiness, you will attract a multitude of women. Or men. Whatever you want! There will be hordes of grasping, fawning sycophants beating down your door, offering up every possible sexual delight and perversion—all you have to do is open the door and point at the crowd! "You, you, and…I think…you." And in they will come, ready to submit themselves to your most debasing whims, the most sordid, sadistic desires you can imagine. And, my friend, you can imagine plenty, because you are grimy with opulence and can afford the many lawsuits that will follow.

There is your reading! And it is absolutely free! Although, considering how extremely, disgustingly rich you shall shortly be, would you like to perhaps make a small donation…?

Fit Loser

Alessandra Rizzotti

JASON, 25 to 29

JASON *walks into a mess of an apartment. More dorm-like than grown-up. He's followed by an old friend.*

JASON   Great to finally have you come over and check out my man cave. I know I've been sorta MIA lately, but I've been really trying to get my life going in the right direction after the breakup with Tammy. She was like my heart and soul, man. But with her porno thing, she was like way too addicted to working. I mean, I'm all for work ethic, but, well you know...it was just hard to compete with the big guys. Not that I'm not big, I'm just no professional.

Watch out—that's my new mini beanbag from Sharper Image. Pretty comfortable for watching the X Games and stuff. It always psychs people out because it blends into the brown carpet and looks like Sheila over there. I LIVE for Sheila, bro. I know she's a Chihuahua, but she's a boss lady. Way better than Tammy, because she listens, if you know what I mean.

Oh you like my new stock of vitamins? I got three cases because you have to take your calcium, fiber, and zinc if you want to be attracting the ladies! It's just that simple. Tony Robbins would agree. Healthy body, healthy mind, healthy relations.

You read that life-coaching stuff? I'm thinking of becoming a self-help guru. When I was Tammy's agent, it was hard to focus on myself, but with the Tony Robbins's lessons, I'm getting so close to being the master of my universe.

[*He starts lifting weights by his window and has a deep realization.*]

I'm thinking I should be the citizen police dude of Hollywood. See that? Prostitutes are always hanging out on the corner causing accidents and stuff. I could stop the accidents before they happen—like I wish I had stopped Tammy before she got into porn. OMG. OMG. Oh my GOD! That could be like my way of giving back to society! It's like I know how it is, ladies. I lived that life as the supporter of sex work. But as my bro Robbins says, "Don't let pain and pleasure use you!" Women get desperate for like fame and stuff. But ladies, "If you can dream it, you can achieve it!" You don't need to do sexual stuff to be famous, even though it helps people like Lindsay Lohan. Instead, be like smart like Natalie Portman, ladies! OMG. That is it! I could be the Tony Robbins of porn stars and prostitutes, bro! I could really make a dent in this world! And like, I wouldn't become their boyfriend or anything. It would be purely professional. Yeah! Oh wow!

[*He lifts a huge weight with a big emphasis on his breath and exertion, then excitedly jumps down to do five quick push-ups with claps in between.*]

Man, you just inspired me without knowing it, dude. You're like my Mr. Miyagi. I should like hire you to be my life coach so that I can be a life coach! You don't have to make a decision now. Just think about it. He-he. Did you still want to go to Carl's Jr., by the way? I'm gonna trampoline after some onion rings. We could shoot the shit and talk strategy and stuff if you want.

Nacho Boyfriend

Kathy S Yamamoto

JOSEPH, 20s

JOSEPH *is an incredibly good-looking man who, though sometimes dim-witted, is hard working and means well. His girlfriend, Tabby, broke up with him the day before, after catching him in bed with another girl. This is the first time they've seen each other since.*

JOSEPH   Hey, hey, hey. Tabby. I know you're mad, but I think I came up with something that will make it better.

[*He pulls out a piece of paper from his pocket and reads from it.*]

Yes, I slept with Annie, Laura, Monica, and Ruth.

I didn't expect for you to find out the truth.

I slept with Ruth last night just so I could make that line rhyme. You should be impressed with my commitment, I mean Ruth is weird. She has that weird eyebrow, and is always talking about her parakeet and the rice at PF Chang's. I mean, I sat through twenty-five minutes of her comparing the rice at PF Chang's to the rice at Kaizuka, before I slept with her. That's how much I love you, babe.

Although, I guess I could've rhymed "Laura" with "horror," though that's kind of a slant rhyme and I wanted to make sure this was the best poem ever, because I wanted to make it up to my girl.

Wait, don't go! I'm not done. I'm being romantic! Isn't that what you always wanted me to be? To make grand gestures out of being so desperately in love? Well I'm desperate now, baby. Because I know I messed up. And I don't want to lose you. So please? Let me finish?

I know that you're mad and you said that you're leaving,
But you gotta know, you gotta keep believing,
That I love you. And that's what I'm saying,
So please forgive me for all that straying,
And all that straying that I'm bound to do,
Because sleeping with only one person gets boring,
Even when that one person is you.

Tabby! Come on! That's only the first stanza. Look, I know that you're mad at me, but I'm just trying to be open and honest! I wouldn't mind if you slept with someone else! As long as you did some grand sweeping gesture for me, like make me nachos, but not just regular nachos with shredded cheese, the kind that has pork and jalapenos and tomatoes in it. Like, you could pretty much sleep with anybody else if you made that for me.

But if you don't like that idea, that's fine, Tabby. Because I will stop sleeping with other girls if that's what it takes. I would do anything for you, Tabby. Really, that's why I wrote this poem for you even though I hate poetry, because I want you back. And I worked really hard. I didn't cheat and go on rhymezone. com or anything because that's how much I care about you. I mean, I guess I cheated by cheating on you, but I didn't cheat on the poem. And isn't that the important part? Here, please let me finish.

So I hope that you know that I truly am sorry,
I hope this poem works, 'cause you said you loved them in your
diary.

I know, that one is a slant rhyme but I really couldn't help
it…Not much rhymes with diary. It's like the "orange" of
books. Nothing rhymes with it! Oh yeah, I hope that's okay
that I did that, read your diary. I was just getting really
desperate and I didn't know what to do. None of your friends
would talk to me about it—which was okay, since I felt weird
talking to them anyway since I slept with them behind your
back.

Although to be fair, Ruth wanted to talk about you, and
although that was super helpful, it only added to her being
weird. I decided to not talk to her, even though it would've
saved me the trouble of reading through your entire diary. Boy,
do you write on the toilet a lot? It seems like you do. I guess if I
were a girl, I'd write on the toilet too, since it seems like you
guys spend so much time on it. You guys are so lucky you get to
sit while you pee, that it's socially acceptable. Man, I'd get stuff
done on the toilet. Is that why you're so productive, Tabby?
Because man, I put off so much other stuff to write this poem,
when I could've been doing it on the toilet if I sat to pee. Or if
I pooped between the time I slept with Monica and now, which
I haven't. Should I see a doctor about that?

Okay fine, fine. Please just let me finish and then if you still feel
like you want to dump me, that's fine. I'll just know I did my
best.

The moral of this poem is that you are my one,
My other half, I revolve around you like a sun.
And I hope with this poem, your heart I have won,

And if not, I'll just have to hang with my bros,
And find another girl to make me some bomb-ass nachos.

Really? That won't make you stay? Fine. I didn't need you
anyway.
Oh my God, I just rhymed, maybe poetry is for me!

Oh no, Ruth. Look, you're very nice but I don't care about the
moisture content of PF Chang's rice! I did it again. I'm a
genius! No wonder all these girls will sleep with me.

Emo Gothic Love

Alessandra Rizzotti

SHAWN, 17 to 23

SHAWN *looks through a telescope, up at the sky. He's a tall, skinny guy who is sensitive, full of love, and a lot of darkness.*

SHAWN   Do you see that? That's Saturn. Cassini is rotating around its rings right now, taking pictures of its surface. Saturn is the flattest planet with the most rings. Seems like a paradox. Like us meeting. We're two depressed people and yet we somehow make each other happy. But not happy in a sappy way. Just in a normal "here we are existing" type of way. 'Cuz you know, being happy is annoying sometimes.

I was really surprised by your text, ya know. I thought I'd have to suppress all my feelings about you and just be your friend like some kinda gay sidekick. But wow—you thinking I'm attractive? I never feel that way. *You're* the one who's really beautiful, you know? Inside and out—as a person. I didn't think I could open up to anyone this way. My biggest fear is saying too much and seeing you abandon me for that. I feel like a douche canoe for saying that. God I'm so lame. . . . No, I really am.

When you said I could come over and take a bath, I wanted to take you up on that. Like I really did want to put cucumbers on

my face and pretend like I was a woman for a night. I wanted
you to paint my nails and tell me stories. Because that felt right.
To be with you, vulnerable, in an intimate, raw way. You said I
have a feminine power and wow, why not embrace that, right?
Is that fucking weird? You know, I've never liked a girl till I met
you. I didn't think I could ever do it, because my mom is such a
bitch that my opinion of women is whatever. I mean, not of
you. You're special. But ya, I've never liked girls. I've never
liked guys. I've always just been asexual. You make me feel
different though.

I got out of the house yesterday just to walk. I never go out. I
saw some geese and ducks, said hey what's up, and I was proud
of myself for taking that step and seeing the sun and just being
my pasty-ass self getting super sunburned. Listening to
mariachi by the park and wishing I was Mexican, when I'm just
a really tall, feminist machismo man that could be mistaken for
a KKK member. God, being in the KKK seems like such an
easy thing to do. Great for stupid people to feel like they
belong to something. Ha-ha...ugh, if only we could feel like
we all belonged somewhere, am I right?? It's hard being smart,
don't you think? I feel judged a lot. I feel like I'll never amount
to anything, when really I have all the potential in the world.

You make me comfortable enough to say that—to admit that I
feel inadequate. [*Starts to cry.*] God...I'm crying like I'm some
kinda emotionally retarded baby. I don't do that in front of
people...but I feel myself around you. I let my guard down and
it feels right to embrace that side of me. The entire world
crashes in front of my face, but I somehow remain calm
knowing I'm here with you.

[*He looks through the telescope.*]

Check it out. Saturn's rings are vibrating through the telescope. It makes me think of holding you tight against my chest. Oh man, here I am crying and all I really want to do is just kiss you. Would you want that? I feel weird asking, "Can I kiss you?" because in my mind, we should both want that, at the same time. The gravitational pull between us should be clear, vocally, you know? I feel it, but do you?...It's okay. I understand. I should probably stop crying first. I'm such an idiot sometimes. But man, you're wonderful. I'd want to date you if you ever felt like that was something you'd want to do.

You would? Wow. Can I hold your hand right now? I just want to squeeze you.

Release Those Endorphins

Matt Taylor

GREG WILSON, 35

GREG WILSON *is a fit and healthy 35-year-old who occasionally drinks far more than is good for him. Intensely cynical by nature, he sporadically mixes bouts of intense physical exercise with lengthy drinking sessions, as he cannot figure out which is better for him—after all, what do trained medical professionals know? Here, Greg is drinking in his local pub with his good friend Adam Garcia. The pair went to school together but Adam is much lazier; he is also famously cheap and often tries to skip paying for his round at the bar. When he complains bitterly about knocking his last beer over,* GREG *loses his cool—there are worse things in the world than spilling a beer.*

GREG   Jesus, you think you have had a bad day just because you knocked your last pint over?! The gym is more dangerous than the pub, trust me. I was in 24 Hour Fitness yesterday and some deranged fitness guru silently challenged me to a treadmill death bout.

You know how it goes. You get on a machine and start on a pleasant, easygoing jog, then suddenly a taller, buffer, and frankly, far better looking guy gets onto the treadmill next to you and gives you that look. That sort of "let us battle for ownership of the virile females in this building" look that only buff, spandex-wearing gym queens throw at people.

Well, actually you don't know how it goes, because your ass never leaves that stool, but trust me, it happens. Usually to short, fat people that start sweating the moment they hang their towel off the machine.

Anyway, he proceeded to ape my movements and speed to the letter, and when I further elevated the treadmill a few minutes later, he copied that, too. At this point, I gave the aggressively domineering male to my left a quick questioning glance, and he inclined his head slightly towards me as if to say "what else have you got, you saggy waste of skin?" As childish as it seems, I rose to the bait and decided to try and show this young upstart that despite having a slightly larger ass and a rapidly retreating hairline, guys our age aren't over the hill just yet.

Ten minutes later, my would-be destroyer and I had ceased any pretense of coincidence and we were essentially locked in a grip of death despite being three feet apart. The next thirty minutes was a genuinely soul-crushing effort. I would rather have been jogging through the embers of my recently burned down house than challenging the guy who stood next to me, but it was too late to back out now. No matter which settings I chose on the machine (that was now the bane of my existence), my leaner, obviously fitter tormentor matched me. And so began an unspoken battle of wills, where neither of us spoke, but we both silently acknowledged that we were savagely butting heads in a battle that first began when our ancestors first crawled from the primordial ooze eons ago.

At the forty-minute mark, my shirt was so wet it looked like I had been blasted off my feet with a riot hose before entering the gym, and I was running up a treadmill that was so savagely inclined that I felt like I was powering up a rubber version of the steep side of K2. I was flailing my arms like a burning break-dancer and smashing my feet so hard into the treadmill that my teeth were slowly vibrating out of my skull, yet still he pursued me. At this point, my heart was hammering against my rib cage and I genuinely thought I was going to faint. This would be less of an issue if we were running through green meadows as God intended, but such an act here would see my vomit and blood-soaked cadaver thrown across the gym and into the free weights area forty feet away. Anyway, for whatever reason, I was still unwilling to do the smart thing and concede.

Approximately four and a half minutes later, just as I was giving up all hope of leaving the gym alive, my nameless tormentor finally gave his head a shake, and then knocked 5 or 6 kilometers an hour off of his machine. I carried on as best I could, desperate to try to show that I was above such a childish display of machismo and we were never really competing at all. I mean, surely because he had instigated the whole thing I could simply plead ignorance and be the better man. I could simply pretend that I regularly went for a peaceful, leisurely jog, and then proceeded to run at a pace that blasted my shins to bits and almost caused me to shit my shorts.

As I slowed my machine down, the sadist to my left gave me a grin, shook his head slightly, and brought his machine to a halt. He then grabbed his towel and his keys, leapt from the machine in a sort of sprightly "fuck it, I think I'll go for a swim instead" sort of fashion, and made his way towards the exit with a fair sheen of sweat but looking none the worse for wear.

The same could not be said for myself, however, as despite feeling merely light-headed when I got off the treadmill, I suddenly felt extremely ill when I stood upon solid ground. I began staggering while simultaneously looking as if I was clutching a pencil between my ass cheeks, and made my way to the changing room quivering like an alcoholic with Parkinson's disease.

Not wanting to faint or vomit in front of any of the other men present, I made for a bathroom stall as swiftly as my recently liquefied kneecaps would allow. Mercifully, it was empty, and I stumbled into a cubicle, collapsed next to the porcelain, and spewed acid and bile into the pan. I then started shaking uncontrollably and drifted in and out of consciousness for about ten minutes before I finally had the strength to operate the door handle.

As I passed the mirrors on the way to the exit on unsteady legs, I caught a glimpse of my pallid, green-tinged reflection, and found myself wondering two things. First of all, if I was the victor of this impromptu battle, why did I feel so demoralized and dejected? And secondly, if exercising is so good for your health, why did I look like a recently reanimated corpse?

I never look that shitty when I sit on this barstool all day.

A Little Fresh Air

Mark Harvey Levine

A MAN, 20s to 40s

A MAN *is at a park. He has a stroller with him. In the stroller is his infant son.*

NOTE: Both the stroller and the infant in the stroller can be mimed.

A MAN   So here we are, getting a little fresh air. We feel you need air. Apparently there's no air in the apartment, so we're out here getting air.

[*Beat.*]

It's interesting. You can get away with a lot in public. I mean, look at you. You can barely sit up straight. You're drooling. You may be relieving yourself right here. You're like a drunk. If I did any of that, on a bench in the park, they'd lock me up. I'd be one of the lunatics, talking to myself.

[*Beat.*]

Oh, God, I am one of the lunatics, talking to myself.

[*Beat.*]

I envy you, y'know. You get the full spectrum of emotions, from absolute devastation to unfettered happiness. Sometimes all in the space of about five seconds. I mean, when you cry, you cry with everything your tiny little heart can muster. And here's me, at my sister's funeral: [*Subdued.*] "Yes...thank you...it was very sudden..." When you're happy, you laugh with your whole body. And here's me, being complimented: "Oh, no, you're too kind." You get to experience heartbreak and pure joy. We get...everything in between.

I mean, I can do without the heartbreak, but where's my pure joy? Why don't I get pure joy? I could use some pure joy right now. Where is it? Where is it? And you get to sit in a park and cry your eyes out, or laugh hysterically, and nobody runs away. Far from it. Women now come to us. Beautiful women walk right up to us. Now, at the very moment when I obviously no longer need them, women are approaching me. Where were you in high school?

[*Beat.*]

Here comes one now. Of course, the irony is, instead of wanting to flirt with them, some bizarre protective gene has kicked in and every woman is now a potential baby snatcher. There are these chemicals in my brain left over from caveman days. A stranger is approaching. Must protect you. Must. Protect. My only chance is to break both her knees and maybe one of her hands before she can grab the kid.

[*He starts talking very fast and serious.*]

She's approaching from the east. If she gets one hand on the kid I can still uppercut her jaw and—

[*The lady says something complimentary about the baby as she passes.*]

[*Sheepishly.*] Thank you.

[*And she's gone.*]

Of course he's cute. He's extremely cute. He's incredibly cute. He's adorable. And I'm going insane. I'm going insane. And you…you're trying to tell me something. What? What?

[*Beat.*]

I have no idea what you're trying to say! But you seem very intent. And you're drooling. Again with the drool. Why do you need so much saliva? You're on an all-liquid diet! Here, wipe your mouth for goodness sakes.

[*He takes a cloth from the stroller and wipes the baby's face.*]

Okay, let go of the cloth. Let go of the cloth. Let go of the cloth.

[*Beat.*]

Alright, let go of my hand. Let go of my hand. C'mon, let go of—Fine. Hold onto my hand, if it makes you happy.

[*Beat.*]

It does make you happy, doesn't it?

[*Beat.*]

Oh. There it is. There it is.

Robert Before the Interview

Chrissy Swinko

ROBERT, 30 to 35

A modern and sparse office waiting area. There are a few chairs and a side table with a bowl of candy. ROBERT enters, wearing business attire and holding his résumé in a folder. He is old enough to know himself and what he is good at, but he has experienced enough that he is super frustrated and lost some of his youthful enthusiasm.

ROBERT   Yes, of course I'll wait. I understand she's a very busy woman. I'm just thankful for the opportunity to discuss how I can contribute to your success. Suugo is on the forefront of technology and I would love to be part of the team.

Yes, I know you're the receptionist.   Hah! That's funny. You're right, I should save my answers for the interview. Thank you.

[*He watches her exit and then sits.*]

Come on, Robert! Idiot! Don't blow this.

[*He takes in a deep breath, then exhales. Deep breath in, then exhales. He looks at his watch.*]

Oh. Of course I have to wait. I'm too early. I should have waited outside. Gotten a cup of coffee. Walked around the

block. Well, I've done it again. Now they think I'm too eager.
Well, I am. I need this job or—I—I—

[*He takes in a deep breath, then exhales. Deep breath in, then
exhales. Takes out his résumé to review it. He puts it back into his
folder. He notices the bowl of candy.*]

No, that's probably not for me.

[*He looks more closely.*]

Chocolates, mints, butterscotches. Huh. Could probably have
one or two before she comes back.

[*He looks at his watch.*]

Wait, no. I know what this is. Suugo is famous for their
interview techniques. It's a test. I bet they count how many are
in there before and after they make people sit in this waiting
room. How come I'm the only one in here? They're probably
watching through that mirror.

Oh no. They've probably been listening to me talk to myself.
Why do I do this? Ruin every opportunity.

[*He takes in a deep breath, then exhales. Takes out his résumé to
review it. He puts it back into his folder. He stands up slowly and
approaches the candy bowl. He very slowly selects one piece of candy.
He looks toward the door as he puts it into his mouth. He grabs
another piece and eats it. He talks to the mirror.*]

 You know, you're supposed to tell someone when they're being
recorded. It's the law the last time I checked. And I'm an
excellent programmer, so really you're the ones missing out
just because I failed your "candy bowl" test. I work with

computers, not people; I'm not good at being "normal"—
whatever that means—

[*He grabs more candy and eats it.*]

I don't understand why I can't just be left alone with my
programs and why do I have to talk to some HR person when I
could just show you if you gave me fifteen minutes with your
coding system!

[*He grabs more candy and eats it. He is startled when the receptionist
returns. He speaks with his mouth full of candy.*]

Hi! Yes, it is very good, thank you. Better me than you? Oh—
hah—that is funny. Yes, I do have an extra copy of my résumé.
Um—while you're here, actually—can I ask you a question
about that mirror?

Hostage Negotiator

Leah Mann

JUDD, 20s

JUDD—*young, handsome, entitled, and vaguely annoyed—sits on the floor of a bank lobby. A bank robber points a gun at* JUDD's *head.*

JUDD   That is that? Nine millimeter? Not much of a gun man; myself—never really understood the appeal. I prefer to fight with my hands. Now the martial arts, that's something. You KNOW your opponent. Hand-to-hand combat is the most visceral game of chess you'll ever play.

[*Beat.*]

Do you have to point that in my face? It's very aggressive. You could point it at my chest, still effective, slightly less off-putting...

[*Beat.*]

...thank you. You look nervous, I'm sure it's going well. Your partner seemed very confident. That's half the battle. Everyone I've ever met who's moved up in the world was a cocky, self-entitled asshole. Nice guys finish last, which makes you a smart man.

[*Beat.*]

Not an insult, you're in good company, not to mention the balls it takes to pull off a heist like this...very impressive. You don't hear about a lot of bank robberies these days. The real robbers are the bankers, am I right? And if it's not some fat cat with a golden parachute cheating you, it's credit card fraud, hackers, that sort of thing. Less threat of bodily harm, I suppose. So respect, from me to you.

[*Beat.*]

Now me, I'm what you'd call privileged, so I never worried too much about money and I'm too lazy to get into finance and do all the work it takes to play the system.

[*Beat.*]

Ransom?

[*Beat.*]

Nah, it's been done before. I doubt my dad would go for it a third time. The second time was already a tough sell, plus, we had a fight last week. Is that another chopper? They're going all out. Someone's getting his fifteen minutes of fame today! Me, I don't like being the center of attention. It comes with so many expectations.

[*Beat.*]

I remember back in the day when I was still hitting the clubs and booze, cruising on daddy's boat, the paparazzi would be all over me and my sisters, mostly my sisters. You couldn't forget your panties or impregnate a socialite without the whole world judging you. The world was a better place before social media and the twenty-four-hour news cycle.

[Beat.]

I'm sorry, am I talking too much? I'm not trying to distract you. I don't do well with silence, and other than that woman's sobbing it's like a library in here. No! Don't point the gun at her, it'll only encourage her.

[Beat.]

And now the gun is floating back up to my face...We can't keep it at my chest? No problem, your call.

[Beat.]

It sounds like it's getting serious out there. Is your partner getting anywhere with those demands? If you let us go—not being pushy, just practical—I could hook you up with a ride somewhere. You could even take the boat out to international waters, or the jet...the jet is nice...anywhere you want as long as the jet comes back when you're done. It's very expensive. Of course, you'd still need a cab or bus to get to the airfield...forget it, too complicated.

[Beat.]

Um, look, I have to sneeze and I don't want to bang my head into that thing and cause a mess. Give me a few inches? Thanks.

[Beat.]

Ahh...Ahh...

[Beat.]

Never mind, it went away. Look, realistically, at this point, you're caught. There are cops swarming outside and probably a

SWAT team getting ready to crawl through the vents, and the longer this goes on, the bigger the consequences. Trust me, once I fake-kidnapped my gerbil to get sympathy from my mom and by the time I came clean six weeks later, little Virgil was dead and all I got was grounded.

[*Beat.*]

I'm not trying to get in your head—like I said, I talk when I'm nervous. Obviously you get real quiet when you're nervous. And other people whimper and sob. All reasonable reactions to an extreme situation.

[*Beat.*]

All I'm saying is the writing's on the wall. In my experience, and this is my third hostage situation, the best way to save your ass is to cut a deal and turn on your partner. Look out for number one, you know what I'm saying? If you don't, he will.

[*Beat.*]

Go on, call the cops. You can use my phone.

[*Beat.*]

My pleasure, man. While you're doing that, do you think you could untie the teller for like five minutes? I really have to withdraw some cash…outstanding debts, and whatnot…

[*The robber whacks him in the head with the gun.*]

Ow! Fine, I'll wait. I should have used the ATM. Just give the phone back when you're done. I have some incriminating evidence of my own on there, if you know what I mean.

Teacher's Lounge

Gina Nicewonger

COACH TANNER, middle aged

COACH TANNER *is chaperoning a class camping field trip. He is talking with a student in the teachers' lounge at the camping lodge.*

COACH TANNER   Hey, Calvin. Having a good time on the camping trip? It is very cold. I'm aware that all of the outdoor activities have been cancelled. Actually, even though I'm a teacher, I do agree that it feels like we are all trapped inside with nothing to do.

"Prison" is a bit extreme, Calvin.

No. I've never been to prison. Do you think they'd really hire me to be a coach if I had? At least they have a gift shop. That's one thing that looks like the website.

I don't know. What'd you get? A sweatshirt?

Geez, okay. I just thought you might want something warm. Neither of us wants to be reminded of this place. God, it's so hard to make small talk with you.

You got a mood ring. They still make those? So, what's you're mood then?

Just tell me if you want to tell me.

Your mood is sensual? Listen, Calvin, I don't know if we should be having a conversation like this. If you have some questions about how your body works or whatever, we can talk, but maybe when more people are around. This is NOT how I was hoping this week would go. Please, don't confess anything to me right now. I don't think I can handle it. Do you even know what "sensual" means?

I think "sensual" means something a little different than "passionate about art" or whatever.

Fine. Fine! You're sensual. But I swear to god, Calvin. If you go home and tell your parents we had a conversation about how sensual you are, I'm going to be out of a job and you're going to end up with a coach you like even less than me. We'll see how sensual you feel when they actually make you play sports in PE.

You're right. I'll never be sensual, and you sure as heck won't ever be a jock. I did used to care about things, you know. Maybe not the same thing you're passionate about, but still.

For Manifred

Leah Mann

HIS MAJESTY THE KING, middle aged

HIS MAJESTY THE KING *addresses his army and loyal subjects from his castle balcony. The* KING *is middle aged and not particularly attractive, but he holds himself with authority. His voice booms with leadership and confidence.*

HIS MAJESTY THE KING   Loyal citizens, valiant warriors, beloved subjects.

[*Beat.*]

Today we go to war. We fight for freedom, we fight for our land, and we fight for love. In the face of darkness, we will be the light. In the black of night, I, your shining beacon, will lead you into the dawn. Some of you will die, and many of you will be brutally maimed.

[*Beat.*]

Some of you will know what it is to send your cold swords into the hot flesh of the enemy. You will watch as the life drains from their eyes and it will change your spirit forever. Others will know the feeling of steel sheathed in your belly, the gurgling of blood in your throat as you desperately try to shove your intestines back into your stomach. You will see your

comrades fall and know your women and children at home are
mourning. Wives, sisters, and daughters will be left to fend for
themselves, to scrimp for food.

[*Beat.*]

Some of your wives will undoubtedly turn to prostitution to
provide for their fatherless babes. Your children may wither
away or find themselves sold into slavery. Your mothers' wailing
will echo through our villages. Our crops will be watered with
the tears of those left behind—as this field is fertilized with the
rich loam of your blood.

[*Beat.*]

In the face of this danger and inevitable suffering, you stand
strong behind me—well, in front of me—steady in your resolve.

[*Beat.*]

Our enemy has affronted us most terribly. Every moment we
wait, my darling jester—bringer of laughter and joy to my
heart—is being cruelly held against his will.

[*Beat.*]

Manifred is well known to you all as the smile that brightens
our kingdom and my dearest companion.

[*Choking up.*]

It brings bile to my mouth to think of our enemies chortling at
his pratfalls; despair to the pit of my stomach to think of his
witticisms entertaining their unworthy masses; and fury to my
brow that the nefarious, putrid King Xander should gaze upon
Manifred's most jovial and perfect of faces.

[*Beat.*]

Those of you who have spent time at court have been privy to Manifred's good humor. You know well how he dotes on your king with the passion of a loyal subject. You've witnessed his impeccable dance moves. Indeed, even the lowliest among you was swept up by the classic choreography he created for my coronation, performing his work with glee around bonfires, thousands of your arms reaching for the sky in unison whilst you jumped and frolicked in celebration of me.

[*Beat.*]

I have my critics who claim this war is a folly, driven by vanity and lust. Their spiteful tongues spew lies of Manifred's fidelity. They say my love's freedom to remain in service to his king is not worth thousands of lives—your lives. But I know none of these critics stand before me today. You are the true of heart.

[*Beat.*]

Today you fight for our shared future. A kingdom is not made up of one man, but of many—and it may not be righteously ruled by one, but by several.

[*Beat.*]

Self-knowledge is second only to love. I am your king, yes, descended from gods and destined to rule you, but I am not perfect. Nay, I am partially human and therefore flawed. My overwhelming sense of duty, of justice, and my dedication to my country have rendered me solemn and at times sorrowful. It is only with Manifred at my side that I can rule as a complete man, a man who experiences love and lightness in addition to the burdens of my position. Would you have a melancholy king?

[*Beat.*]

No! Would you have a king with an empty heart?

[*Beat.*]

No! Would you leave your kingdom without its very soul?

[*Beat.*]

NO!

[*Beat.*]

And so today you fight. You tell our enemy that we will not be stomped on! We will not be stolen from! We will have our joy back no matter the cost! Stand in front of me and face the swords and arrows of those that would darken our lands! Let your hearts be pierced by spears so that mine may be full once again! Today we dive into battle full of courage, our spirits lifted as we rise up and shout—For king! For Country! FOR MANIFRED!

About Mom

Eitan Loewenstein

CHUCK, 40s

CHUCK, *who lives in Middle America, stands in front of his teenage son in the family room of their home. He gestures for his son to sit.*

CHUCK   Son, sit down. No, not there, that chair is almost about to break. Not there either—I just washed those cushions. That's fine, just watch your elbows. Tuck 'em.

[*Beat.*]

You probably noticed that your mother isn't here having this conversation with us. Normally, for things like this she would be, but not today. Because she's dead. Really dead. Just keeled over right in that chair.

[CHUCK *points to the second chair.*]

That's why I had to wash it. You understand. Now you probably have a lot of questions about your mother and death. Well, I came up with a few bullet points I think will answer most everything. Number one, there is no afterlife. Your mother has no soul. Every part of her is completely gone except for a cold hunk of flesh that is now laying in the earth. Which brings us to number two: you missed the funeral. It was this morning. I was going to wake you up, but you got in pretty late last night so I let you rest. Number three...Nope, that was it. Oh, you're probably wondering how she died. It's a funny story. Well, not for her. Or for us, really. It was cancer. Or a heart attack. I always mix those two up. A moment of silence.

[*Beat.*]

Alright, on to new business. Since your mother is gone, I figure I should start dating again. Not today, obviously. I need some time to plan and get a haircut. Maybe next week. I've prepared...

[CHUCK *pulls a piece of paper out of his pocket.*]

...a list of your ex-girlfriends I'd like to take a run at. If there's anybody on this list that mentioned how sexy I was in passing or seemed to have a thing for older men...just put a little check next to their names.

[*Tries to hand the paper to the son, who doesn't take it.* CHUCK *puts the paper back in his pocket.*]

You can get that later. Like I said. No real rush or anything. It's not like I have cancer.

[CHUCK *pauses and looks at his son.*]

You seem upset. Distraught even. That seems fair. She was your mother. Although, if I'm able to give some constructive criticism, being sad that your mother has died is a bit of a cliché. You're a very unique kid; I was just hoping that uniqueness would extend to your grieving. But hey, that's the fun of parenting. Discovering new things about your kids every single day.

[*Beat.*]

I got a coupon for a free game of bowling. We could go, take your mind off of this whole death thing. I know, it's a big scam since you still have to rent shoes. I mean, where else in the universe do you rent shoes? Can you imagine? Driving is free, but you have to rent a car!

[*Beat.*]

I already cleared her stuff out of the closet. You should see how big it looks now. It's amazing. I can separate my suits out from my casual stuff. I'm going to be much better dressed now that I can see all of my clothing at once. Which is important because I'm back on the market. I have to look my best.

[*Beat.* CHUCK *really thinks about what he's been saying.*]

Huh. Wow. Maybe this joy, these plans for the future...maybe I'm just covering up the deep pain of losing the woman I love. This isn't right. This isn't how a person is supposed to act. I'm sorry. I should have been...oh my god. This isn't how you needed to hear about your mother's passing...it's not how I should have...I'm sorry. I'm so sorry...

THAT I WAS KIDDING! HA! Oh my god, the look on your face. The look! You were so sad! Like when you were a baby and I broke your fire truck. The saddest! You cried for hours. Your mother isn't dead! For real. She's alive. She just left early this morning for work. Lighten up.

But she does have cancer.

New Roommate

Gina Nicewonger

JESSE, 20s to 30s

JESSE *is showing the house to a potential roommate. They are talking in the kitchen.*

JESSE   This, obviously, is the kitchen. So as you can see, it's a pretty cool place to live. We're five, hopefully six, grown men. Respectful, laid-back, mature men. And everybody's really fun too, but I don't want you to think it's just a party house. We're all adults. Seems like the keg's not tapped. If you want some, help yourself.

Anyway, none of us really thought we'd live in a communal living situation like this after college, but you know, living in a big city is expensive. You and I would share a bathroom. It's through that door. I wouldn't go in. It's a little messy. You know how it is. I thought I'd clean it after work, but it actually takes a while to scrub sharpie penises off of all your toiletries. Yes, I said *all*. There's literally a penis on everything I own in there. That's true dedication, really. We're a real committed group of mature guys.

So your room is the one at then end of the hall. It does come furnished. No bed. Just a hammock. I've heard it's great if you have any joint problems. Don't be ashamed to admit it. All us mature guys understand. Surprisingly, not an issue for bringing lady friends over, either. They go in and out of this house like you would not believe.

Anyway, like I said. We're hoping to fill the room by the end of the week and we really feel you'd fit in. Clearly, you're also a nice, mature guy who doesn't have a criminal record. If you did, that would be bad, right? Because between you and me, the cops are here a lot.

The Cook

Tanner Efinger

ANDREW, 39

ANDREW *is the head chef in a busy, well-respected restaurant. He's worked in kitchens for twenty-four years and, as many chefs do, he has a problem controlling his temper. He is currently in a therapist's office speaking to a therapist about his rage issues.*

ANDREW   I don't even know why I'm here.

I mean. Yes. I know I'm here because I was forced to...Alright, fine. It is required of me by my employers to resolve my anger-management issues. I'm not angry.

Hey. Don't look at me, pal. This is just the industry. When I was a young chef I was bullied. And my head chef was bullied when he was starting out, too. It's a vicious cycle. I didn't say it was fair. It just is.

What did I do?...I hit the kitchen porter with an eggplant.

Look. I can't expect you to understand. You work in a pillow. You talk about feelings in an air-conditioned office with all the comforts of heaven...what is this? A stapler. Yea.

I don't just cook. You know? I don't just throw some Tater Tots in the oven and squeeze some ranch dressing into fucking ramekins, you know. I'm an artist. An artist in a high-pressure, hot, highly criticized, did I mention hot, environment. I deal in burns and cuts and sweat and knives and flame. And you? You deal in staplers.

The pressure? You want me to talk about the pressure? Fine. It comes in bursts. And when it comes, it smacks you in the face like a frying pan. Ticket after ticket after ticket. Sautéed scallops, chargrilled pigeon, Icelandic salted cod, squeeze of lemon, shoulder of suckling pig, pickled vegetables, bacon popcorn…Are you writing this down? Because I'm not done.

You want to talk about pressure? Pressure is table forty-one, unhappy with their coconut ash pudding. They say it's too "squidgy." And they don't want something else. They want it less "squidgy." And while you are trying to understand how to make a fucking coconut ash pudding less "squidgy," a thirty-seven dollar steak is dropped to the floor by the waitress who you think might be stoned. And then another ticket. A table of sixteen and they are all, all of them, having burgers. Six of them are medium rare, three are medium, four are medium well, and three are cooked well done—though why on god's earth you would want to pay fifteen dollars for me to burn meat is beyond my ability to understand humanity. Two no pickles, one no onion, three no buns and replace the fries with salad, one of those salads has no dressing, six cheddar, one blue cheese, and don't forget about the coconut ash pudding, and the steak on the ground, and the salted cod, and the pigeon and ticket after ticket after ticket.

[*He slows down then, a pang of guilt.*]

And then…then you just snap. You don't even notice as you grab the eggplant and it flies across the kitchen.

And later…I want to apologize. To say I'm sorry. But no one ever said sorry to me, so I don't know how.

You want me to pretend that you're the kitchen porter?

I'm sorry. No really. I'm sorry.

The Orchid

JP Karliak

PAUL, late 20s to early 40s

PAUL *is meeting up with his longtime friend Brian at the local watering hole. He is very excited to introduce his gorgeous girlfriend Courtney to Brian. As to why he's excited…well, that's something else.*

PAUL   Courtney? Oh, she's great. Just great. How are you? [Laughs.] No, she's great. I'm really excited for you to meet her. You'll never believe how hot she is. I mean gorgeous. Like way out of my league. And spontaneous! You never know what she's going to do next. One minute she's quiet and unassuming and the next she's ya know, right?

[*Beat.*]

She's screaming at imaginary leprechauns for stealing her taco salad. No, really, she's crazy, nuts, bonkers, lost her marbles, threw the brain in the blender and hit Puree, God help us. But, I digress—she's hot, so what's a little crazy, right? And she's funny! Did I mention how funny she is?

She's a riot. Like, last week I bought her an orchid…a potted one, so it'd last. She's always said she liked them, so I figured why not? I'll get her one. So I buy this dark, dark purple one with a really nice pot…plastic but the marble detailing is very nice. And I give it to her, and do you know what she does? She stares at it like it's a Chia pet giraffe, sniffs it—not like people sniff flowers but like a dog sniffs dead animals—and says, "This is shit." Isn't that hilarious? She's got this sort of dark, dry, almost cruel sense of humor. Like the British, exactly! Anyway, she's puts the orchid on the TV and leaves it there for three weeks.

Three whole weeks. On her TV. Unwatered. Untouched. So, big surprise, it starts to wilt. And yeah, I admit, that hurt my feelings. How many guys do you know that actually pay attention when their girlfriend says what floral variety she likes, let alone actually buys her flowers? The most basic upkeep would have been nice, I mean, a plant needs water like a...like a man needs...I dunno, fuck metaphor.

Anyway, week three, when I ask her if she's going to water the plant, she gets a little testy, as if it's my job to not only gift the gift but to care for the gift as well. Which is so her sense of humor. Like it was my fault it wilted! Or, even funnier, like it was the dog's fault! Oh, poor Buster, why? [*Weeps.*]

What? Buster? Oh, he's fine, he's...visiting relatives. Anyway, she gets passive-aggressive and just dumps a glass of water on the orchid.

Now, I dunno if you've ever experienced this, but sometimes when you dump water on really dry soil, the air escaping makes a little squealing sound...nothing loud or weird, but it's kinda high-pitched like [*makes noise*] or [*makes another noise*]. Well, neither of those really, but you get the idea. So she hears this and goes apeshit. "Oh my God, listen to it! I water it once and I kill it! It's screaming because I've killed it! You son of a bitch, look what you made me do! You made me kill it, you motherfucker!" And she's screaming and crying and starts throwing a fit, and I'm just stunned, when all of a sudden she says, "I won't let you stand there and watch it die, you bastard!" And she hurls it at me! She picks up that heavy marble-esque pot and heaves it right at my head! Luckily, I managed to jump behind the couch or it might have killed me! She might have ended me right there, that fucking sadistic... [*Beat.*]

... ally funny woman! Taking the jokes to the limit. I mean, it's not like she really threw the plant AT my head, she was just kidding. Even when I was sprinting out the door, she was saying something about having orchid blood on my hands. Orchid blood. See, that dark, cruel humor? God, she's funny. Hot and funny. How do you beat that combination?

I'm just shocked she's with me. I mean, I'm not her type at all, we look so weird next to each other. You'd probably look better with her than I do.

Oh, here she comes. Look, I have to run to the... bathroom, but you guys order, don't wait for me. And, uh, remember I told you that if you went after one of my girlfriends again, I'd kill you? Yeah, that was harsh of me, you just be you, okay? See ya!

Night Before

Lynn Trickey

MATT, 20s to 30s

MATT, *dressed in pajamas, opens his hotel room door, and finds a woman standing in front of him.*

MATT   Wow. Wow…you're here. Not going to say part of me didn't think that maybe you might come…but really? The night before your wedding?

No wait, before you say anything. I saw the way you were looking at me at the rehearsal dinner, Cindy. I felt it. And I know you were thinking, "Damn, Matt looks good these days, is he working out?" And yeah, yeah I've been going to cross fit. But I'm not one of those people who has to always talk about it, which is probably why you didn't know about it until now, because I'm into it, but not, like obsessively—

No wait, let me finish. What we had…I never felt like it was done. I'm still in love with you. I have been since college! And you started dating Dave so soon after we had that weekend together, I didn't think it would last. And I honestly thought that once you realized that he was totally wrong for you—I mean he wears *fedoras*. How could you take him seriously? No, that was rhetorical. I figured once you had some time to find yourself, you'd come, well, not *crawling* back, but maybe *slinking*, or at least sheepishly walking…

No let me finish! The point is—it's too late. I'm sorry. I mean, if you had come to me at the engagement party.... Okay, truth time? I only brought Tricia to make you jealous, I know you find her obnoxious, and actually I can't stand her either, but I knew it would get your goat—I was waiting for you to come to me that night. And if you had showed up then, I would have said, "Yes, break it off, let's get out of here and never look back..."

But now? Now? Shhh, LISTEN! You're not thinking! You have a dress, we're in the Hamptons, I paid a LOT of money for this hotel—by the way, do you know if breakfast is included or...no, never mind, not important, I can figure something out...

You have a honeymoon planned to Boca! What, are you and I gonna go instead of you and Dave?

[*He pauses for a moment, and considers this.*]

I mean is that even possible anymore? To transfer tickets to someone else's name? The hotel wouldn't be a problem, but the flight—

No, stop, I can't. It's too late. I'm sorry. Maybe, *maybe*, once you guys have been together for a while we can discuss, you know, if you are going to have an open marriage, or if you and I want to just hang as friends and see what happens physically...

[*She finally interrupts him. He listens.*]

Huh? My wallet?

[*He reaches out and takes his wallet from her.*]

Oh. Yeah, I guess I did leave it someplace...I was wondering why I couldn't find my hotel key...

[*Beat.*]

So... that's why you came here tonight?

Ah.

But... But you were staring at me at the rehearsal dinner?

[*He reaches up and feels his face, wipes something off of it.*]

Oh, fuck. Marinara gets everywhere—WHY DIDN'T YOU TELL ME?

I'm not yelling!

No I'm not.

NO I'M NOT!

I'm not mad! In fact, all that stuff I said? About being in love with you? That was... that was... well I was just saying that to make you feel better. Because I knew you had these feelings for me...

Yes you do.

Yes you do!

No wait. Don't go! Wait. Honestly... Don't you ever think about it? About us?

Come on, not even a little bit?

Oh please, it's so totally clear that you're in love with me.

Yes you are.

YES YOU ARE!

You're only kidding yourself!

NO, I'll see YOU at the WEDDING TOMORROW.

NO, YOU DON'T MAKE A SCENE!

NO, YOU STOP YELLING!

NO, I'M GONNA GO!

I KNOW THIS IS MY HOTEL!

YEAH, GOODNIGHT TO YOU TOO!

[*He opens his wallet, looks inside.*]

Hey, I had twenty bucks in here!

A Toast

Leah Mann

LOGAN, late 20s to early 40s

LOGAN, *a slightly rumpled playboy, is standing in a wedding reception tent. He is dressed in a tux, with a glass of champagne adorning one hand and a microphone in the other.*

LOGAN Wow, look at all of you. I did NOT realize we had so many relatives. I know you didn't all come to my wedding.

[*Beat.*]

Probably for the best, that was a bust. Kept the presents, though. Didn't keep much dignity...but that juicer has stood the test of time.

[*He chugs from his glass.*]

Down to business. Ellie's been my little sister ever since she was born.

[*Beat. No laughs.*]

Nothing? All right.

[*Beat.*]

It was always just the two of us, and even when she drove me crazy, and goddamn, did she—for three straight years I asked

Santa to take her away instead of bringing me stuff—but I always loved her. She had that little-sister thing, where I hated her half the time but wanted to keep her safe and happy outside of whatever torture I was inflicting.

[*Beat.*]

She'd fight back, too, completely baffled why I was nice to her in public and a terror at home. Her big heart didn't get it—she either liked you or not. No games.

[*Beat.*]

Ellie wasn't as book smart or sharp as me, and frankly, she could be lazy, but she was smart enough to learn from my mistakes. Every time I got caught smoking weed, sneaking booze into the house, or "borrowing" the car, she'd watch silently and take notes.

[*Beat.*]

Ellie's superpower is her ability to do just enough for her life to make it smooth and easy. It's an impressive sixth sense about how to direct her energy. She never got in trouble for anything. Which was bullshit, but I can't blame her for being clever. I might not be a role model, but at least I'm a lesson.

[*Beat.*]

Which brings us to marriage. Once again, Ellie seems to have learned from my mistakes.

[*Beat.*]

Tony here is a great guy. He pays his own rent and he doesn't appear to be a herpes-riddled cheater, which is definitely a plus. Some things really are forever, am I right?

[*Beat.*]

I am right.

[*Beat.*]

These two, though, they'll be forever in the incurable love and happiness way, not sexual disease way. Ellie gets what she wants and she knew Tony was the one from the first time they met.

[*Beat.*]

Look how their eyes are all sparkly at each other. It's cloying but very sweet and this is a wedding, so hooray for love!

[*Takes a big swig of champagne.*]

Yup. Love. Fucking awesome.

[*Beat.*]

Awesome, at least for our newlyweds, and I mean that sincerely. The good news is Ellie's life is not mine and god willing it never will be.

[*Beat.*]

My life is a work in progress, having recently deleted my marriage and started rewriting myself. I'm working on a solo show, at the moment. Ellie and Tony are beginning a new chapter in their...romance novel....Not that I'm dwelling on the titillating sections.

[*Beat.*]

It's about finding your own path. Sometimes those vows you say before family and friends and god are just a big fat check that your future self won't want to cash. You won't be married to the same people in ten years. Everything changes. It's the only constant of the universe.

[*Beat.*]

If I could give you two any advice, it'd be to stagnate joyfully together.

[*Beat.*]

If you do decide to expand your horizons, do it together. Definitely do NOT spend a month in the desert doing peyote and meditating without each other, because that'll throw off whatever kind of groove you've got going.

[*Raises his glass.*]

To Ellie and Tony. Whether you grow or stagnate, may it be together; may you cash your checks in ten years from well-padded accounts of love and happiness. I'll keep making mistakes, if you keep learning from them. Starting with that bridesmaid—Tony's cousin. Where'd she go?

Nicole

Mark Harvey Levine

BARRY, 20s to 40s

BARRY *is in a giant retail store. He is energetic and friendly.*

BARRY   I love this store. I just love it. Well, I love going to aisle 14. Aisle 14 is where all the dolls are. I know, I know, a grown man going to the doll aisle.

You think I'm some kind of sissy—or worse, a perv. And I'll admit, sometimes I'll say I'm shopping for my daughter, so people won't think I'm a sissy, or a perv. But I'm not shopping for my daughter. I don't even have a daughter.

I'm there for the dolls. Well, one doll in particular. There's a nurse doll—just one—that I like. No, no, let's be honest. That I love.

And she loves me, too. I mean, it's not like I'm stalking her or anything. I just go visit with her. I tell her about my day, my stupid office job. And she tells me funny stories about the doctors she works with, or an interesting patient she had that day.

I don't get to see her often, because of my work schedule, and because of her schedule as a nurse, and the store's schedule. Well, I know you're open twenty-four hours, but sometimes late at night they restock, and there's this huge stack of boxes in front of Nicole.

That's her name, Nicole.

But today I manage to squeeze around the boxes and the wall and—she's not there. She's not there. I can feel my heart going a mile a minute. I try not to panic. Maybe I misunderstood her schedule, or she had to work a second shift to fill in for another nurse who got sick.

But my real fear was—what if someone bought her? What if some little kid had picked her up—or worse—some man. Some man who really did have a daughter. What if they had purchased my Nicole?

While I was having heart palpitations, I bent down to catch my breath and—there she was. Visiting some of the…more modern dolls. She was telling them that they were very pretty girls, and they shouldn't feel like they have to dress so slutty to attract boys.

She's like that. She's always been a role model to the younger dolls. They look up to her, and not just because she's on a higher shelf.

As I picked her up and began cuddling with her, I started to worry. Nobody had purchased her this time, but what about next time? She was beautiful. Who wouldn't want her?

I would have to hide her. I would have to hide her someplace nobody would find her. I could stick her in the stack of surplus grass seed over in Home and Gardening. But they might find her. They have people who do that, you know. Just wander through the store taking back the shampoo that's in

Electronics, or the box of cereal that's sitting among the towels.
I always wonder if those are things that other people have
loved, and tried to hide away.

So I had to stick her somewhere where I could get to her, but
no one else could. Men's Shoes? Hardware? None of these
seemed like a good place for Nicole.

But then it hit me. I could…buy her. I could just buy her
myself. It was so obvious that I never thought of it before.
But—would it cheapen her? Paying for her like she was some
common hooker? Nicole blushed, but looked at me and said,
"Free me, Barry. Free me from this polyurethane and
cardboard cage. Take me home with you. Take me home."

And for $15.97, plus tax, she is mine. And isn't that what
America is all about? You see something in the store, you fall in
love with it, you buy it, and take it home.

So could you ring her up for me?

The Newlywed

Leah Mann

VIJAY, 20s to 30s

VIJAY, *a handsome young East Indian man with a light British accent, loosens his tie as he approaches his new bride. The interior of the honeymoon suite where they are staying is swanky. VIJAY seems comfortable in the expensive surroundings.*

VIJAY So...hi. This is even weirder than I thought it'd be. No offense! You're not weird. I mean, maybe you are—if you are, that's okay. Eeesh, awkward. I don't know. That's the whole point, isn't it? We don't know each other. I guess it's time to start?

[*Beat.*]

Do you want to go first?

[*Beat.*]

No? Okay. Fine, totally get it. No pressure. You can even leave the veil on. I'm curious, of course.

[*Beat.*]

Eventually you'll take it off, right? To shower or eat. Not that it matters what you look like! I'm not superficial like that. Your face does not define who you are or how happy our marriage will be. Maybe you don't like my face—it doesn't mean you don't like me. Do you like my face? Is it okay? I've been told it's nice, but it's so hard to tell if people are just being polite.

[*Beat.*]

Alrighty, let's start with an easy one. Just dip a toe in, so to speak. Favorite color? Any food allergies? You a reader? I love reading. Probably too much.

[*Beat.*]

Right, sorry, that was lots of questions. Pick any of them.

[*Beat.*]

Orange? Nice choice. Bold, bright, I like it. Mine's green, that sort of dusty gray green of pine needles—that's my favorite. Smells good, too. Not that colors smell, but you know how you can imagine what a color would smell like, my green would be misty and a little mysterious. Orange would be fresh and zesty. Do you ever think about stuff like that? What pictures would sound like or what a song would feel like? Some people can actually do that—synesthesia. I can't, but I try to imagine it. What's your favorite song?

[*Beat.*]

You don't have one? Not a music person. Huh. Okay. Not everyone is. Nothing wrong with that. I'll do one—"Hey Jude" by the Beatles, you know that one? Who doesn't? That song would feel like thick, velvety moss on a gray day.

[*Beat.*]

Do you enjoy the outdoors? I adore them. Being outside mellows me out. Sometimes my brain gets a bit manic, like a merry-go-round spinning about too fast, but if I'm outside I slow down and can get off the ride for a bit. Something about the wind and the sun and all those smells seep in and rinse out my head.

[*Beat.*]

A romantic? I suppose you could call me that...this isn't very romantic, though. More a business deal, really, to make mum and dad happy, isn't it? It's all so archaic, but you hit a certain age and after years of denial you succumb to the family pressure. I didn't find anyone on my own, did I? So fine, we'll grow to love each other like our parents did.

[*Beat.*]

Your parents hate each other? Sorry to hear that. Tragic. And you still agreed to this? They paid for your university? Yes, and they want grandkids of course...that's a ticking uterine clock. A deal is a deal, I guess. I admire you for sticking to your end of the bargain. My parents don't hate each other. They're quite fond of each other, actually—it's rather impressive. I'm optimistic.

[*Beat.*]

You're more of a pessimist? I always say, it's not being pessimistic, it's being realistic. Ha-ha-ha. And realistically, you're right—we might dislike each other more after we get familiar. It's a distinct possibility.

[*Beat.*]

Getting distincter by the minute.

[*Beat.*]

Sorry? Oh, my mistake—"distincter" is not a word. "More distinct." Thank you for correcting me. I'm always happy to better myself. You're improving me already! I've never been much of a grammarian. More of a math and sciences guy myself.

[*Beat.*]

Not to be blunt, but it's getting late and tomorrow there will be all sorts of questions...so where do you stand on this whole wedding night business?

[*Beat.*]

I don't want to pressure you, but we are man and wife now and you did mention getting a move on with children.

[*Beat.*]

I'm quite good. Not that I have loads of practice, but enough. I'll certainly do my best to please you. I'm not a selfish man as far as that goes. I take pleasure in a woman's pleasure, so that should be a point or two in the plus column. Make up a bit for the poor grammar?

[*Beat.*]

Have you ever had any practice? Just out of curiosity...not asking in a judgy way. Good, good, we're on even ground then. So perhaps we can start with your veil. Call me a traditionalist, but I like to see a woman's face before I see her...everything else.

[*Beat.*]

No? Goodness, of course you can keep the veil on. I wouldn't want you to see me cry, either.

[*Beat.*]

I'll just stop asking you questions and disrobe so we can get you started on those kids.

[*Beat.*]

You're welcome. Happy to oblige my new wife.

Bro Vow

Chris Quintos

LUKE, late 20s to early 30s, bro

LUKE *professes his love at the altar for Lisa.*

LUKE   I didn't write anything down because I wanted to speak straight from the heart. [*Beat.*] Lisa—I've loved you since the moment I saw you at Club Rain. It seems like just yesterday you were standing across the dance floor with a lychee martini in your hands. You are the sexiest, most beautiful, hottest woman alive. My very own Megan Fox. Time passes so quickly. I can't believe it's already been eight weeks. And now we're here, on this beautiful beach, getting married. In front of all of our friends and family.

Well, most of our friends and family. The ones who weren't already busy. I mean, um, the ones who really matter. I promise to always be true to you. I promise to love you with all my heart. I promise to always get water for you in the middle of the night. I promise to always text you if I'm going to be late. I promise to keep in really good shape for you.

I promise to always be on time picking you up from your manicures and to remember that it's a nonfat VANILLA latte, not hazelnut, that you like. [*Laughs.*]

I can't believe we are going to have a baby. I mean, I really can't believe it. But I don't want you to think that I'm marrying you just because of that. I'm marrying you because I love you, and because I want to spend the rest of my days with you. There's no one I would rather be with. No one I would rather wake up next to. No one I would rather work out with. For real. You keep track of all my reps without complaining, and you never lose your place. You always make sure I look good, and that my car looks good—and I know we both think that's important. Because how can you trust someone who looks like a slob? And it's important to be with someone who has the same values as you do. I saw that on a talk show once. I think it was *Oprah*. And as everyone knows, Oprah only speaks the truth. And, I just, I can't believe how lucky I am.

You are the best workout buddy, outfit consultant, and now wife, and soon-to-be-mother that a man could ever ask for. I'm lucky to have you. And in the immortal words of Edward Cullen, who I am a poor placeholder for, "I promise to love you forever, every single day of forever."

Phone Calls

Jeff Passino

SCOTT, 30s to 40s

SCOTT *is in his office, in a textile plant.*

SCOTT [*On the phone.*] Right, right... well the one thing I know is if you had chicken pox, the shingles virus is already inside you.

[*Dave walks into* SCOTT*'s office and sees his boss is on the phone. Dave is about to exit, but* SCOTT *motions for him to stay and sit.*]

[*Whispering, with his hand over the mouthpiece.*] I'll just be another second. Sit down.

[*Back on the phone.*] HA-HA-HA-HA-HA, oh my gosh, I hadn't heard that. So funny...

[*Dave leans in to find out what is so funny.* SCOTT *shoots him a look as if to say, "Shut up, I can't hear."*]

[*On the phone.*] I'm sorry, what did you say?... Oh yeah! My wife does that all the time... Uh, no, I'm not married... Well, I imagine it from time to time...

[*Dave starts to stand up and gestures towards the door, trying to say, "I can come back later."* SCOTT *waves him off and points to sit back down again.*]

[*Whispering, with his hand over the mouthpiece.*] I'm almost done. Just one sec.

[*Back on the phone.*] What was that last part? I couldn't hear again. Well, someone's being loud…oh, I don't want to—like three feet…same thing he's always wearing…uh huh… maaaayyybeeee…well, I don't…oh YES, he DOES and I HATE it.

[*Dave is uncomfortable and tries to ask if* SCOTT *is talking about him.* SCOTT, *of course, waves him off as if to say, "Don't be silly."*]

[*Covering the mouthpiece.*] We're talking about a different Dave entirely.

[*Back on the phone.*] I think he's starting to put two and two together, better just get to business…Yes, I have the PO right here. [SCOTT *opens a notebook in front of him.*] Ready?…It is FGD 135…FGD…F…F as in "Foxtail"…G as in "Gravy train"…D as in "Re-DEMP-tion"…and then 1…135…no, just one 1…135…not 1135, 135…right, but put a 1 before it…before the 35…right, that's it, and then…oh no, the FGD is before the 135…FGD…It was, I just told you this…F as in "Footloose and Fancy Free"…G as in "Oh Gee, Mr. Wilson"… and then D, which rhymes with The…135…You got it?… Read it back to me…Where did that 2 2 come from?…Oh right, that wasn't part of it, that was…Yes, I can smell it from here, but that wasn't, that was before I…There you go, drop the two 2s…Okay, great…It was good talking to you, but I should go now, what's that?…Oh yes, I definitely will.

[SCOTT *hangs up the phone and turns toward Dave.*]

Now then, Dave—let's you and I figure out a way we can reduce our storage bills. Mint?

Teeth or Testicles?

Matt Taylor

RICHARD FITZPATRICK, almost 40

RICHARD FITZPATRICK is almost 40, and he is as bad at poker as he was when he first started playing as a teenager. RICHARD is playing a game of poker in his kitchen with four of his friends, the most pathetic of which is his neighbor Chris Jones, a man so cowardly he refuses to visit the dentist and has not been for a checkup in over a decade. Unfortunately, he has had toothache for two days and has a dental appointment tomorrow. After Chris has talked about nothing else for the past hour, RICHIE has decided to educate him.

RICHIE   I actually can't believe that a man your age is afraid of the dentist. We are trying to enjoy a leisurely game of poker, and you are pissing and whining because you might need a filling tomorrow? Jesus! At least that guy is stuck working on your mouth and nothing else. If you want to get worked up about a medical practitioner, you should worry about the doctor; he gets to play around with your nuts. Ask a guy whether he wants his teeth or his testicles messed with, a smart one picks the teeth every time.

Shit, I heard that once you hit fifty, it is normal for them to jam a few fingers up your ass to check your prostate! And some guys even have female doctors. Can you imagine that? I wouldn't want a female doctor looking at my fucking feet, let alone thrusting a few well-manicured fingernails into my back passage.

I hope that's just my old man yanking my chain.... My doctor is a lumbering giant from the Czech Republic or Poland or somewhere and he has fingers like goddamn bananas. He speaks to me as if I was some sort of illiterate asylum seeker who just arrived from the Himalayas, and he talks to me in pigeon English despite the fact it's the only frigging language I know. I went in last month to get a whooping cough shot before we visit the in-laws in California because my wife swears it's rife there, and he acted like I had just told him I was going skinny-dipping in Angola and tried to jab me with every needle in his office.

Oh yeah, and when I jokingly asked him about booking my mother-in-law in for a CAT scan he looked at me like I had just dropped my pants in front of his kids, so I suspect that he has no knowledge of some of the most common medical procedures in the developed world. I have no idea where he went to medical school, but it wasn't anywhere they practiced on humans. He was probably a veterinarian in Kazakhstan and he decided to pursue a new career because all of his dogs kept dying.

Honestly, the guy terrifies me. I wouldn't trust him with a pair of plastic scissors let alone a scalpel. If I had appendicitis or something and I had to choose between having him treat me or just dusting the crumbs off this table and letting a lumberjack goad my organs with a pitchfork, I would pick the fucking logger.

Anyway, the absolute worst thing that can happen at the dentist is that he pulls the wrong tooth or something, which would suck, but they can fix that kind of shit easy these days. Did you see the state of Nicolas Cage back in the early nineties? He had a set of teeth like the ones you see on a string around a witch doctor's neck. Fast-forward ten years and he has those big ass shiny Hollywood teeth; looks like he could eat an apple through a tennis racket.

If your doctor fucks up, you might end up leaving his surgery in a bucket.

You should forget worrying about your teeth and lay off the whisky and cigars instead!

Women's Lib

Alisha Gaddis

CLINT, mid-30s to 40s

CLINT *likes to hear himself talk. He is sitting in a recliner and has just been asked a question to which he replies.*

CLINT   Feminism. Wow.

You know what the worst part about a feminist is? All of it. I mean—the whole concept is ridiculous. I am not antifeminist. I just don't think it affects me. I was born out of someone's vagina with a dick. I am a man. I am not a Wo-Man. This feminism crap is not my fight.

I mean—is some hairy-armpit megabutch woman gonna start yelling at me about how women don't get equal treatment? I mean—is Susan Sontag gonna pop out of the bushes and tell me I'm a jerk? Is someone gonna show me a pamphlet about teen brides?

It's not that I don't think women don't deserve the same as men. But feminists—feminists just want to oppress the man. All men. Push 'em down and rise above 'em. And why would I want to oppress my own kind?

I just don't have the bandwidth for that bullshit.

I do not have time to care about what feminists want. Do you want me to walk out on the corner and pass around a petition asking for ladies' boobs to be on display while they breastfeed their kids? I don't want that. Cover that shit up! No one wants to see your dark nipples and saggy breasts. I just want to see big tits on the Internet from the privacy of my own couch. Use a cover!

But I get it. I love women. I have a mother. I have a sister too.

But I am not going to march in a parade just because I think some chick should make the same thing as me. Maybe if they worked harder (or wore a shorter skirt to work), they would make a few extra cents on the dollar. I mean—am I right or what?

But, I think I am a progressive guy. I cook. I let her drive.

But listen, if I try to open the door for you and you say, "No, I got it"—then bitch, please—I am not going to open it for you again, and you can buy your own drink! Am I right?

But I get it. Women wanna be like men. They want to be the same. But they are WOMEN. We are MEN.

Let's just be honest—feminists are ugly ass woman who no one wants to marry anyway. THAT is why they are so angry.

But if you want to do your report on feminism, sweetie—I think that is a great idea. Daddy supports you 100 percent— now can you go grab me that remote over there? My car auction is on TV and you're blocking my view.

Tony Joey

Tammy Jo Dearen

TONY JOEY, all ages/every man

TONY JOEY is best summed up as a chauvinistic douchebag. TONY's strong East Coast accent, manicured goatee, and slicked-back hair is his signature winning combination. Fist pumps and leg kicks punctuate his social commentary shout-outs and declarations. He is a disgusting pig that speaks louder than his elevated voice.

TONY JOEY   I don't understand lesbians. I call them women who are more challenging to fuck. I said it! Boom. Over the top!

And…What's this "no means no"? Women don't *know* what they want. They don't *know*. They can barely read.

I said it! Hey!

When a woman says "no," I hear "I'm thinking about it!"
BOOM!
Cuz I *know* what they really want.
I'm Tony Joey. Everybody wants a piece of this!
HEY NOW!

You wanna see a magic trick? Huh?
You wanna see a magic trick?
I can split a woman in half…WITH MY COCK.
AIR RAID!!! BOOM!!! And the crowd goes wild!!

It's hard to find a woman these days. They're so fat.
They got these Natural Woman campaigns for fat chicks...to
feel better...about themselves...cuz they're fat.
I don't want them feeling better about themselves.
Who wants that?
Clean my house! Bring me a sandwich. Blow me!
I speak for everyone here.
And Plus size? What's the plus side? Plus what? Plus I'm not
fucking you!
Boom! HIT ME! She's got a full house!

Skinny girls. I like skinny girls...My kind of girl is the girl
that asks,
"Do my shoulder blades make me look fat?"
HEY!

You know what it's like fucking a skinny girl?
It's like fucking a deflated blow-up doll.
Where's the hole?!
Heyah! Killin' this!

You wanna see a magic trick?
Huh? You wanna see a magic trick?
I've seen Chaz Bono naked.
Now that's magic!
She's not a man.
She just got so fat, she went to the other side.
HEY! Biggest Loser!

I fucked this Asian one time. I do favors. Her pubic hairs were
straight like the hairs on her head. I put 'em in two ponytails
and I was like "Hello Kitty." HELLO KITTY!
Where's my puffy sticker?!

I fucked this earthy girl.
She used stones for deodorant and she still smelled.
Maybe use some Mitchum, maybe some Right Guard?
Maybe some Secret? Cuz I got a secret, you stink.
P.S. P.U.!
Say it with me! P.S. P.YOU!

I fucked this old lady one time.
I fucked this old lady.
Philanthropist.
She was so old her eggs were rushing down to meet the sperm.
It was like the man who never came to dinner.
I opened her legs and it was like CAVIAR?
This bitch is classy.
Who's got a cracker?
Can someone get some champagne up in this bitch?
HEY!
I'm Drivin' Miss Daisy.

My mom was just in the Senior Olympics. Who cares?

You want this?
There's a line to get in it. I'm like McDonald's—over 100 billion served.

Boom!

Hey, I think this is going pretty well for a first date. You wanna come up to my place? BOOM!!

Coney Island

Tanner Efinger

A MAN, mid-30s to 40s

A MAN *gets on the subway.*

A MAN   Excuse me. Wow. Crowded! Pardon me. Pardon me.

[*He holds on to the railing above him and smiles at the woman who is sitting down near him.*]

Excuse me. Do you know if this goes to Coney Island? It does. Oh good. All the way to the end of the line. Got it. All the way to the end!

[*He laughs at that. Beat.*]

It's my first time. To Coney Island—not riding a subway. I've done that before. Lots…I've always wanted to go. Since I was a little boy. Have you been?

Oh sorry. You're reading.

[*Beat. Another passenger bumps into him.*]

Excuse me. [*Smiles at the passenger.*] I'm going to Coney Island today. I saw a picture of the Ferris wheel when I was a kid and I imagined sitting at the top, looking over the water and wondering if I could see the North Pole. You can't, obviously. I

mean I know that now. You can probably see the Bronx or
something, right? Or Staten Island? I don't actually know much
about New York geography. Or maybe you can't see anything.
Just water as far as the eye can see.

Oh, this is your stop. Okay. Excuse me...Bye!

[*Another Beat. He looks at the woman reading her book. He smiles at
her.*]

You can't put off your dreams, you know! I've learned that the
hard way. If you want to go to Coney Island, you should go.
Right? Because suddenly your thirty-seven with a wife and a
three-year-old living in Ohio. OHIO!

How did I end up in Ohio?

Is it a good book? I haven't read it. I haven't read very much in
the past decade, to be honest. I should read more. And drink
more water. And go to church. Quit smoking. I know I
should...but Life, man! Am I right about that? Life!

[*Beat.*]

I left them, you know. I left my wife and my three-year-old.
Her name's Thomasina. My daughter.

Come with me to Coney Island! I know it sounds crazy. We
barely know each other—okay, we don't know each other—but
have you ever been before? See! You've never been and you've
never gone on the Coney Island Ferris wheel.

Come on, I'm offering you a day of adventure. Let's do
something crazy. We'll ride the Ferris wheel, have a Coney
Island hot dog—I hear they are infamous—for being big, or
particularly hot doggy, or something.

And then let's get a hotel.

With two separate beds!! I didn't mean that. Really, I didn't. I meant that we could disappear from the world for one night. And we'll tell each other secrets and prank call the lobby and fill up the ice bucket for no reason whatsoever. I wonder if they have a candy machine. A candy machine. Can you imagine that?

I know it's silly. I know. I've got my kid and you've got your...book.

All the way to the end of the line.

[*Another passenger bumps into him.*]

Excuse me.

Excuse me.

Excuse me.

Baseball

Rachel Raines

TONY, 18 to 25

TONY *is addressing his attorney.*

TONY   Okay, so here's the thing. I wanted to do it. I mean that, I WANTED it the way all children want things, like, really really intensely wanted to play baseball. I wanted it so goddamn bad I was willing to kill myself over it.

I played like crazy. Every day I got home, got my shit, my ball, my glove, and if my dad wasn't back from work, I threw a ball against the side of the garage until he got home. (Mom never woulda let me bounce that fucker off the house, woulda ruined the siding. I don't know anything about siding and I doubt my dad cared, but Mom did and that was that.) He got home and we "played catch." I think that's so fucking funny to say now, we "played catch." Because, yeah, technically that's what we were doing. But come on, kids play catch. Little Leaguers play fucking catch. I was *training*. Even when I was a Little League little shit, I was *always* training. By the time I was in seventh grade, I had to stop practicing as much because the doctor actually told my mom I was gonna blow out my shoulder.

In seventh grade.

I was *twelve fucking years old*. That's how intensely I wanted this.
I was seriously gonna be a ball player and there was no backup
plan. My folks actually banned me from playing. They said "just
for the summer." So ya know what I did? I hopped the fence of
the field and played anyway. Ran the bases. Sprints, ya know? But
I got caught. I actually got caught a couple of times, and there
is nothing better than watching a spare tire jiggle away on some
rent-a-cop trying to keep up with you when you have been doing
sprints for an hour. One day I came home and my mom noticed a
big fucking tear in my shorts. I felt like an asshole…I had caught
them on the fence running from a guard with a beer gut bigger
than my parent's wraparound porch. I had to lie to Mom and I
was scared shitless for a few days that he would show up. I didn't
know then, that tubby bitch was more embarrassed than I was.

I don't have a lot going for me, even then I didn't. I wasn't, ya
know, "promising." Like, there was this kid on the team when I
was, shit, like sixteen or something, and he was fucking magic at
chemistry. He awed people in class with that shit. He was the dick
that did the "volcano" project but made goddamn Funyuns erupt
from the top as a surprise. And he was a damn good shortstop,
never missed a catch. That kid could be somebody. Point is, he
was promising. He coulda done something even if he hadn't
done ball. Fuck man, I even remember the guy they rotated in
for him, that kid *always* missed shit. Like, constantly let hits fly
through his legs. It got to a point where other teams knew to
swing low 'cause if they popped one off close to the grass, he
was gonna fucking miss it. Guaranteed, they'd get somebody
on first. That dick let a ball pop between his knees one day
when he was making the jack off symbol to the third baseman
'cause he had told him he'd fucked his sister. Kids, ya know?
And that kid teaches fucking English or something now. *I* was
never gonna do anything other than pitch. That was it for me.

So I played some college ball, but the fact was even though I was really fucking good, I just didn't get *seen*. I was constantly gettin' that glazed-over, unimpressed shit look from scouts. I dunno why. Still don't. I was good. Really really good. My batting average was better than anyone's.

Ya don't realize it's over until it's over. My grades tanked, no one was interested in recruiting me, and suddenly, fuck, cut from the team. Dropped out. So yeah, I was pissed. Really pissed. But ya gotta understand, I was pissed *for a reason*. There was literally nothing else I wanted to do.

So there, that's it. I tried to smash the goddamn coach's knee with a bat and he *fucking deserved it*. I thought about it first...I used a wooden bat for less damage. He would heal, and you can still coach with a busted fucking knee. Scout after scout never noticed me and I know it was him because I was really really good. He never played me when the big guys came through. He constantly pulled me right when I was hitting my stride. He told me to "take it easy." Are you fucking kidding me? Why would I want to become some pudgy fucking asshole like him? So I did it. I feel bad, felt bad when it happened, but I don't regret it. I'm not a monster, but I got a sense of fucking justice, ya know?

He tackled me. It fucking sucks to say, but he did. I was crouching, which I thought would give me the advantage but it didn't. He saw, he tackled. So next fucking thing I know, three goddamn cops have me pinned ass up to the ground and I suddenly realize if this shit gets photographed and put on the goddamn Internet, I am gonna look like some ass-up dumb-ass.

Which, of course happened.

It didn't help I was high and holding a burrito.

Three Minutes

Meryl Branch-McTiernan

AARON ANDREWS, 29

AARON ANDREWS, *athletic, is talking to a friend on the phone at his girlfriend's Brooklyn apartment.*

AARON   Three minutes is a long time. When you're waiting in line at the post office with a Vietnam vet behind you muttering to himself, or watching Portugal tie with the U.S. in the final three minutes of the World Cup game, or walking through an ally in Harlem at night, it's a long time. But waiting three minutes for Gina's pregnancy test to determine the rest of my life is interminable.

We bought the test at Duane Reade this morning. Or actually, I bought it. I insisted. Making our way down the Family Planning aisle, I looked across at the feminine hygiene section for the first time. From the look of it, owning a vagina required as much maintenance as owning a car. We debated the merits of each test and decided to go with the cheapest one. Gina's period was only a week late. If it didn't come for another few days, maybe it was worth the splurge.

One pregnancy test and one six-pack of Coors Light. I smiled at the cashier and said "Thank you, Belinda." I'd never called a cashier by her name before. Somehow it seemed appropriate today. And I wondered what Belinda thought of us. If she had kids of her own. If she assumed we were a happy couple who wanted to hear the news that we were pregnant. That a positive test would be a cause for celebration, a chance to whip out special cigars saved from our wedding.

Belinda didn't know that Gina and I weren't married. We had started dating three months ago after meeting at a friend's party. At first, I thought maybe she was the one. She was smart and pretty with cleavage that I could poke all night. Neither of us had dated anyone for a while and we were both kind of hoping to find that person who would be our plus one at the billion weddings that thirty-year-olds had to budget for.

Last week, it sunk in. We weren't growing closer. After we spent the first couple months telling each other our childhood stories and our pet peeves, we ran out of topics to talk about. We watched *My Cousin Vinny* together. A classic she'd never seen. She didn't laugh. I looked at her face when Joe Pesci came out in his orange suit. Not even a smirk, a smile, nothing. She always looked bored. Even when we were having sex. Especially when we were having sex. The only time she smiled was when she scrolled through her Facebook feed. I was gonna break it off on Tuesday. And then she texted me and told me she had missed her period. I made a bad joke about how that was a problem, since she was an editor. She found that less funny than Joe Pesci.

After we bought the test, I suggested we stop for bagels. She was in a rush to get home. I was in a rush to turn back time. So we went back to her apartment, which always had the faint scent of cat litter. It made me sad. When I met her, I thought I would save her from being just another thirty-year-old cat lady.

But now I didn't want to save her. I didn't want to have anything to do with her cat or her ovaries. I just wanted to go to Prospect Park and play soccer with the guys. If this was the consequence of sex, I wanted no part in it.

We opened up the test together. I read the instructions carefully, like it was a new board game, with challenging rules to be mastered. "Well, I guess I'll go pee now," she said. I asked her if she wanted me to join her in the bathroom. We didn't have that kind of relationship, but I wondered if the circumstances changed things. "I'll be fine," she said. I cracked open a beer, and asked if she wanted to chug it. To get the juices flowing. She shook her head and I wondered if that meant she was keeping the baby. If there was a baby.

There was no way she could raise my son in this tiny studio. He'd choke on cat toys and stumble over empty bottles of flavored Absolut. Not that my place was a better option. My three roommates were not into joining the Babysitter's Club. Why was I already calling it my son? I guess I'd always wanted a son.

When I grew up.

But I forgot to grow up. My father's accountant still does my taxes. I'd never bought my own car. Or had a threesome. It is way too soon to be a dad.

Three minutes has ruined my life.

So, I guess this ten-minute wait for a table isn't so bad . . .

The Rise of Everyone, the Fall of Me

Jeff Passino

JEFF, 27

JEFF is an aspiring writer who is living in Los Angeles but working way outside the industry he wants. He has always taken a more passive approach to his life, but as all of his friends finally start having noticeable successes in their lives, JEFF has to learn to put his all into what he wants in order to dig himself out of the hole he now finds himself in. The setting is JEFF's apartment.

JEFF   There's one phrase I always heard growing up. From my mom, dad, teachers—other adults who, evidently, had no idea what to say to me. They'd say, "Jeff, you've got so much potential." Sweet thing to say. Of course, they'd never elaborate on it. I mean, potential what? A potential first-round draft pick...good. Potential serial killer...not gooder. And my mom, especially, would tell me she doesn't care what I do with my life as long as I'm happy. Which is one of those things a mother will say to you over and over as you are growing up, but then as soon as you are making decisions for yourself it quickly turns into, "Oh. So you're not going to finish college then? You'd rather move across the country to Los Angeles. Well that's just fantastic."

Now I've always been a reasonably happy guy. And the last five months? Fantastic. A steady job, the most incredible girlfriend. Of course, it's not like the job is actually IN the career that I want…And Karen has been pretty busy the last few weeks with auditions. So, do I exaggerate to make myself look better than I am? Yes, maybe. But just because I want to be perceived as a happy and therefore likable guy, and just because I may not be *as* carefree as I would like you to believe (as I would like to be), that doesn't, necessarily, mean I am *not* a happy and likable guy. And you *will* notice I did say "reasonably" happy, so I am not completely trying to be misleading. Hey, I'm someone who will post a picture of me bored at jury duty on Facebook so that it doesn't look like my life is all fun parties and beautiful hikes in Griffith Park. Admittedly, it took about twenty selfies before I got a "bored" picture I was happy with posting, but…uh. I feel like I'm straying away from the point I was trying to make, which was…what was I saying? I may potentially have ADD. Oh yeah, my job, Karen.

Just because I hope that things can always get better or progress does not mean I'm not appreciative of what I have. How many double negatives did I just use? Like I am aware that I live in a nice apartment. It is very spacious, rent controlled, and in a safe neighborhood. But I'm also aware my roommate is a complete weirdo. I know what I have and when I have a good thing. Or had. I swear I'm not a pessimist! *My life is going to shit.*

See, I just turned twenty-seven, which I would have assumed was too young for a midlife crisis, but evidently not. And so now, more than ever, I need to live up to whatever that "potential" is. That's if I even have any potential, 'cause if not…how do you tell your mother she's a liar?

Therapy Breakup

Gina Nicewonger

GRANT, late 20s or 30s

GRANT *wears his heart on his sleeve and thinks every girl is "the one." However, he's never had a real relationship for longer than a year. He's broken it off with many girls.* GRANT *thought therapy might help in his search for love, so he started seeing Dr. Jill Mitchell over a year ago. He thinks his therapist is good at her job, but like all his romantic relationships, he believes he and the therapist are missing the "magic" needed to be effective.* GRANT *wants to follow Dr. Mitchell's advice of "trying something different" and has come to her office to tell her in the only way he knows how he won't be returning to therapy.*

GRANT   Listen, we need to talk. I know we always talk, but we need to really talk. Don't you hate those words? They're almost as bad as, "It's not you. It's me." But in this case, it's not you. It's totally me.

[*She speaks.*]

I guess I can't hide anything from you. I'm awfully sorry, but yeah, I'm breaking it off with you.

[*Moved.*] This is what makes it so hard. You know me so well. And you get me.

[*She speaks.*]

I know I didn't have to come down here to tell you that we can't be together anymore. I know. But come on. We've been seeing each other for four years. I'm a better guy than that.

[*She speaks.*]

[*Smiling.*] No, no, no. I DO understand that you're my therapist and that our relationship is "strictly professional." But, Dr. Mitchell, I don't know if you understand how much you've helped me get through some really tough times.

[*Laughs.*] God. We've had some good times, haven't we?

[*She speaks.*]

Jill, I've got to stop you right there. Is it okay if I call you Jill?

[*She speaks.*]

Stick with Dr. Mitchell? Fine. Dr. Mitchell, do you know I've been seeing you longer than I've seen any other woman? You're so encouraging, but at the same time you see through all of my bullshit. And the best part thing: you always laugh at my jokes. God, I'm going to miss your laugh.

[*She speaks.*]

I'm sorry. I must be coming off as a crazy person. And, I'm trying to tell you that you're so good at your job. I'd hate for you to think I'm just now becoming crazy!

[*She laughs.*]

There's that laugh. You're an amazing person. But, sometimes you just got a branch out and try something different. Someone very wise once told me that.

[*Getting emotional.*] God Brian, don't get choked up now. Change is hard. I think I told you that one. But hey, we're both going to be okay.

[*She speaks.*]

Oh, you better. I'm going to treasure the invoice for this session for a long, long time. Please. Think of me fondly.

Fuck Yes

Alessandra Rizzotti

LUKE, 43

LUKE *is meeting Kate, a girl he's had a crush on for a long time, at her apartment, to eat dinner. Problem is, he's already in a relationship. He sits down and takes a deep breath.*

LUKE   Oh man. You've caught me just when I've been trying to make things work with Jill for the last three years and it's one of those things where I never felt a spark ever, so why am I even trying? It's such a gray area. I don't even feel anything for her in the passionate sense. I literally look at her and think, "You'll do." And I want to have babies real soon. If I wait any longer, they'll be mentally disabled.

I remember looking at you in the hallway at work and just wanting to stare every time. I would tell my office buddy that. I'd be like—there is this girl at work and I just want to rape her... but in a good way. Like with my eyes. UGHHHHH.

You really like me, Kate? You do? That kills me. Why were we always in relationships? Why didn't we stop those relationships and just say, "Fuck yeah—let's date now!?" I mean that was my thought process, at least. I guess I was scared. I also thought maybe you were too young. I wasn't sure what was the right thing to do.

And I don't fuck around, Kate. I don't. I'm a faithful person. I don't sneak around. So...you're opening Pandora's box. I mean, I need to think about this. I'm going to have to keep you posted. Hopefully I don't have to keep you posted longer than a month. I don't want to think too hard because I have always felt a spark with you and I don't think I've ever felt that with someone right away. I would have babies with a firecracker like you. I mean, you better get ready in a year, because that's my plan.

I don't want to freak you out by saying this, but I seriously would make you my wife. I want to spend my life with you. Getting to know you every day. And I don't think we need to necessarily share the same interests to do that. Love is about a methodology. You like honesty, you like being open, you like being sensual, you're drawn to touch. That's all the love I want. Is that what you want? I feel like three dates and I already know. Do you feel that? If I don't kiss you now, I'll regret it. And I need to calculate all this data to determine if a future is possible. So, come over here. I gotta scientific method our chemistry.

[LUKE *kisses her.*]

Wow. Oh man. Oooooo. I love the way you kiss. I love how you move against me. I'm so nervous to tell you this, but I want to be honest because you said that was important to you. Oh man...this is hard. Okay...here goes. I have herpes. The genital kind. Is that okay? Ugh...so lame. I am such a dummy. And I want to have unprotected sex, obviously, because of the baby thing, so...is that too much pressure? I'm all like—"Fuck yes" about you, but I totally get if you're like "Fuck no" about me. Think on it. If you need a week, I'm totally down for you to process that. But just know, people with genital herpes need love too.

Ha-ha…ugh…you're so beautiful, you know that, right?

Man…What I would do to you.

Let's Be Friends

Eitan Loewenstein

STEVE, late teens to early 20s

STEVE, *bro-ish, walks in the front door of his apartment. His roommate is already chilling on a sofa in the living room.*

STEVE Oh my god. I had a day. A day! You know that girl who always sits next to me on the bus… Tiffany? Right. She's supercute, she's funny, she's got a job. Prime dating material. Except for the whole riding the bus thing. Well. Alright, today starts off great. She saves me a seat, as per the usual. No horrible smells in the air, no homeless people giving me the stink eye. Total romance opportunity. I've got this awesome breakfast burrito, but they screw up and give me bacon. I pick out the bacon and offer it to her. So she's laughing at me for not eating pig, which I don't really appreciate, but whatever. We're both cracking jokes. This is like Meg Ryan–level stuff. So I give her the old, hey, I've got a sofa and a copy of *Transformers* on Blu-Ray. Why don't you come by and I'll protect you from the Decepticons? and she gives me the old, let's be friends.

That's actually what she said. Let's be friends. Those have to be the worst three words in the English language. I honestly think it's more painful than when that girl said, "man, that's small." At least there you had genetics to fall back on. With the friend thing… What? I'm on my own. But it's not even true! She doesn't want to be friends.

We're not going to be sending each other Christmas cards, talking about Bundt cake recipes, and swapping paperbacks. We're just two people who will never see each other naked. Friends. Look at me. I take the time out of my day; I build up the guts that it takes to ask a girl out. I'm shy. This isn't easy. I've got social anxiety issues. They took years to work through. And this Tiffany has the balls to say... well, you know.

That's bull. Man, you know me. I'm honest. I don't play it like that. If I don't want to date someone, I tell them. If I think your poetry sucks, I tell you that your poetry sucks. If I think a girl's fat, I will tell her that she's fat. I mean, not to her face. She'd kill me. But I'm honest. There is something about wearing a dress that makes it impossible to tell the truth. That's why my dad and I never got along.

Am I the only one who listened in third grade? Honesty is the best policy. Mrs. Shando. But she was a woman, so maybe she was lying about that. Maybe it's not the best policy. Maybe there's some other policy that's even better. I should look her up online. Ask her.

I've got all this free time now, since I'm not dating Tiffany.

[*Beat.*]

This day has sucked. Sorry for bitching. I'm done. I'm going upstairs to watch a movie and go to sleep.

[*Turns to go, pauses, turns back.*]

No, you know what? That's not right. I'm telling you the truth. I'm going up to my room, I'm going to watch porn, and I'm going to fantasize about your sister and I'm not going to lie about it. Do you know why? Because I am a man.

Bathroom Smiles

Meryl Branch-McTiernan

JOSH SHAPIRO, 32

JOSH SHAPIRO, *small and wiry, is talking to a couple sitting next to him at an Italian restaurant in New York.*

JOSH   You guys look happy. Taking bites off each other's plates. Are you gonna split a dessert? The crème brûlée looks fabulous. I never get dessert. For a single person, it just seems decadent.

I'm actually on a date. She's been in the bathroom for ten minutes already, and I'd like to finish my meal while she's gone. But that might be awkward. Would it? Is she taking a dump during dinner? On a first date? Or does she have some kind of Clark Kent/Superman thing going on? As I sit here, watching the mozzarella on this chicken parmigiana congeal, she's actually flown out the bathroom window and is saving some old lady from a purse-snatcher.

No, she's not Superman. She's probably on the phone with her friend, Lexi, or "her girlfriend" as she says. I hate it when chicks call their friends "girlfriends," because I get all tripped up for a second. Your girlfriend? Does that mean you're gay? Then why am I dropping money on your second cosmo? We get it. You have a friend that's a girl, but if you're not eating her out, she's not your girlfriend.

She's probably telling Lexi that I fudged my height in my OkCupid profile. The difference between five seven and five nine is negligible. But it opens up the door for me to meet women who are "6"s and let them decide for themselves whether or not two inches matter. And why should she care? She's barely five feet.

I don't get why women love the bathroom so much. It's like their power center. They go in with fuchsia lips and come out with plum. Sometimes they even have couches in there. For what? In case you want to read a book while inhaling the sweet aroma of farts?

My sister tells me that when one chick passes another on the way into the bathroom stall, they smile at each other. Why? Reassurance? Don't worry, I didn't take a dump. I was just changing my tampon. And I never sprinkle on the seat, 'cause I'm a lady. That smell is not my fecal matter. It was somebody else, someone who didn't smile.

There's no eye contact when I pass another dude on the way into the bathroom. I'm busy praying to God that he's a shy guy who uses the stall to piss. Maybe that's the difference. We know using the stall only means one thing.

Now you see these trendy bars with coed bathrooms. I don't like 'em at all. The other day I was washing my hands at the club and the girl next to me, who was pretty hot, couldn't figure out how to get the automatic sensor thing to work. I helped her. But I felt like I was turning into a woman. Everyone was smiling at each other in the mirror. The bathroom is not a place where I have to be "on," where I have to be thinking about flirting with hot girls.

I wonder if I should order another gin and tonic. It'll be my third. I wrote in my profile that I was a social drinker, whatever that means. I mainly drink with friends, except when I'm home trolling Facebook alone. Drinking while using a social network counts as social in my book. I forget how often she says she drinks, but it's got to be more than "sometimes." I never message girls who say they drink "sometimes."

If she doesn't come back before I catch the waitress's eye, I'm ordering another. Maybe I should just date the waitress. I wonder if she'll be happy to serve me when she's off duty. I've never dated a waitress before.

If you asked me ten years ago if I would ever have to resort to shopping for girls online, I would have laughed in your face. I don't even like ordering books off Amazon. But at thirty-two, you start to worry. Is this gonna happen for me? I'd love another decade of bringing girls home from bars. But the truth is, in the blink of an eye I'll be forty-two, and then I'll be fifty-two, and one day they'll stop coming. Won't they? I don't want to find out. So that's why I'm here, staring into my empty glass, watching my chicken harden, while BeachGrrl87 is partying it up in the bathroom.

So how did you two meet?

Bored Barista

Carla Cackowski

BARISTA, 20s to 40s

A BARISTA stands behind a counter, waiting for customers that aren't coming. Eager to please, this guy has a hard time being alone. There is one other person, unseen by the audience, sitting at a table in the coffee shop.

BARISTA   You writin' a screenplay? Uh. I said, "You a writer?" Or are you just Facebookin'? Ah. E-mails. Lots? Wow. Can I be your assistant? Just kidding. I'm kidding. I mean, unless you need an assistant. In which case, I'm serious.

[He takes a sip out of a can.]

Red Bull. Yeah, I can't drink coffee anymore. Doesn't work. I'm too tough for it. I'm a machine and the only oil that gets my engine runnin' is the Bull that is Red.

[The BARISTA whistles a tune.]

You're in here all the time. This is like, your office or something, huh? Kidding. Except that, well, it's kinda true. Nah, fine by me. Especially during the slow hours. I'm cool with it. You want a refill? You sure? On the huz-ouse. Huh? The house. For free. On me. Want it? Sweet!

[*He runs over to the table, picks up the customer's coffee mug, runs behind the counter, pours the refill, runs back to the table, drops the mug on the table, stands there. Waiting.*]

~~You are welcome~~! Anytime, my man. Any. Time.

[*The* BARISTA *still stands there.*]

Mind if I sit?

[*He sits.*]

So how's that dog of yours doing? Yeah, dog. Wasn't that you who has the dog that comes in here sometimes? No? Huh. I must be thinking of somebody else. This other guy has a dog, damn cute dog, named Benny, no, uh, Lenny. That's not right either. Bonzo. That's it! Yeah, Bonzo the dog. Damn cute dog. *Cut* Ever thought about getting a dog? ~~Me neither~~. I imagine taking care of a dog is like taking care of another person. Who has time for that? Not me, my friend, oh no, not me.

Mind if I stand?

[*He stands.*]

~~I got this lower back problem~~. Cannot get comfortable for too long, you know. Mind if I ask you a personal question? Where'd you get your T-shirt? It's tight, man. I like it. ~~Nah~~, I mean I like that it's tight. Good for you. ~~Not many dudes can pull that off. Just a T-shirt? Nah, man~~. That shirt's a lady magnet.

[*He tries to high-five the customer. It's awkward.*]

Aw, sorry! You gotta get back to work. I get it. I gotta get back, too. To work. No problem, man. Just know that if you need anything, I am mere steps away from making it happen for you. I got your back.

[*The* BARISTA *goes behind the counter. He whistles another tune.*]

Hey man, want a scone? No. You sure? A croissant? Bagel? Granola? Macaroon? Beef jerky?

You gotta go? Ah man, don't go. Please don't go. You gotta go. I understand, man. Sure. See you later, brotha. Don't worry about me. I'll just be...here.

Craven Saint Todd

Brandon Econ

CRAVEN SAINT TODD, 28

CRAVEN SAINT TODD *would prefer not to discuss the period in time prior to his being sired and taken into to the cult of Nosferatu. His entrance into this world was fraught with much darkness and light— mostly light and light burns (get it away, get it away, hiss, hiss!). And please do not bring up his two older brothers, Van Saint Todd and Helsing Saint Todd; they always tease him and steal his black eye shadow (which* CRAVEN *steals from ULTA, but still . . .).* CRAVEN *loves anything by Anne Rice and enjoys eating Nutter Butters while hanging upside down from the rafters, which he can only do for so long before the blood of his victims (maybe?) rushes to his head.*

Here, CRAVEN *is talking to his new neighbors, Chris and Susan Brown, on their doorstep.*

CRAVEN SAINT TODD   I hope I'm not interrupting. I saw you unloading boxes, so I figured I'd stop by.

Hi, I'm Craven Saint Todd, I'm a vampire. I mean, not really. But I am a vampire. So, I live next door to you. I guess we're neighbors. You know. So I just wanted to come over and clear the air. Is this your wife?

Hi, nice to meet you. I'm Craven Saint Todd. I'm a vampire. Well, not really, but, you never know. Oh wow, Chris and

Susan Brown. What a great name for both of you. Wow, yeah.
Lemme give you the rundown. Well, so this IS a really family-
oriented community, it's pretty quiet around here normally. It's
really great, you know. But sometimes me and my brood have
these monthly gatherings. I wanted to make sure that you knew
that. I don't want to get started on the wrong foot. You know.
The person that lived here before, total ass. I mean, he would
call the police on us every time we would have our simulated
slayings. It got really bad morale-wise. We would plan things
months in advance, you know. Find an actor on L.A. casting
and everything. So I just wanted to let you know that we do
that sometimes.

Oh, yeah it's this thing we do. Well, we just run through the
neighborhood and chase down an actor, corner her, and then
drain her life force. I mean not really, but, usually.

I just had a thought—you and Susan should totally come over
for dinner one night. Well, yeah, when you get settled in. I love
to entertain new guests. I make some of the best Mexican food.
You would think I was a real Mexican instead of a vampire. I
mean, yeah. You two could stick around and I could introduce
you to my cohorts. Usually every first Tuesday of the month we
have a traditional Mexican dinner and masquerade ball in my
backyard. We all dance and drink and listen to Gregorian
chants. You know, just relax and share in the joys of being a
member of the living dead. I mean not really, but, well? So that
would be fun. You would be surprised how...

Oh, you have a cat—put it away! Put it away! I'm just joking,
you know. Well you have to lighten up a little, Chris. Me and
my coven do that sort of thing all the time. Some of us get
really into it. I remember last week. Alana brought over real

human blood. Well it was Pinot Noir, but you know what I mean. We were passing it around like in a real blood-rite and some of us just, you know, went on a rampage in the community and were jumping on cars and chasing children and I found a rock and I threw it. It got really crazy. When I woke up the next morning, I had wine stains all over my jabot. You have no idea how difficult it is to get that out. We just really let loose. But we have a lot of fun, really. Really!

Well, I've talked your ear off nonstop. I better let you get back to unpacking. It was nice talking to you, and think about my offer. We'll probably see each other again. Like in the middle of the night when I'm standing over your bed ready to suck you dry. I'm only kidding, but, well, maybe. Bye.

Morty Weinberg

Andy Goldenberg

MORTY, older man

MORTY, *a crotchety older man, raises his hands, stopping a kid from complaining about his phone's reception.*

MORTY Whoa, whoa, whoa. What's with all the noise? This is a Target Superstore, not a city hall. We should be so lucky to shop at a place that has daily discounted prices on wrapping paper, office furniture, and bathroom essentials. Before you were even a twinkle in your mother's eye, people had one good that they sold and whatever they charged, that's what you paid. And nobody specialized in wearable video cameras and neon pink flip-flops. What are you so angry about? How can you be mad in a magical wonderland of knickknacks, figurines, and cleaning utensils on generous markdowns. Look at the lighting in here! It's so friendly and fluorescent, calling out to you, like God on high, saying, "Step right up to the super savings. Get 'em while they're hot. While Supplies Last." We only have a limited time here on Earth, not to mention only one hour on the parking meter, and it's just a waste of all those precious minutes to be upset. What's that? They're out of your phone? Oh, the new iPhone. The phone's got a name. We should be so lucky to even have a phone. Our ancestors had to yell as loud as they could, and if nobody heard them, they didn't do anything.

You know, before schlepping all this way, you should have stayed at home and searched their inventory on the Internet. We should be so lucky to even have the World Wide Web and not have to step outside of our warm and cozy houses. Those who came before us had to round up all their earthly possessions into a wagon whenever they needed to come into town and it wasn't a balmy seventy-six degrees outside. It was unforgiving winters where you lost members of your tribe just to make a toilet paper run. And it wasn't super comfortable two-ply. And they sure as hell didn't have any adorable T-shirts with cartoon unicorns on them. Nine ninety-nine? That's a steal! Target? I just hit the bullseye! Are you kidding me? We have it lucky! [*To employee.*] Not you. [*Reading his nametag.*] Alex from Tarzana. You? You work for minimum wage, five times harder than my tottela. He's a plastic surgeon, two years out of medical school, with a beautiful wife and a baby with the cutest little punim. You. You need a little more luck in your life. Speaking of which, is there a way to get a quick price check on this Doctor Dre compact disc? It was in the value bin, but it's still got the original price tag.

Contributors

These monologues were written by actually funny people. Here is their business of funny:

ALISHA GADDIS is Latin Grammy Award–winning performer, humorist, writer, producer, and performer based in Los Angeles. She is a graduate of New York University's Tisch School of the Arts and University of Sydney, Australia. Hal Leonard/Applause Books published her first book, *Women's Comedic Monologues That Are Actually Funny*, in 2014. Subsequently, she signed on with them to release five more books in this series, including the book you are currently holding in your hands. Her columns have appeared in College Candy, Comediva, *GOOD* magazine, and Thought Catalog. She is the founder and head writer of Say Something Funny…B*tch!—the nationally acclaimed all-female online magazine. The highly irreverent Messenger Card line that she cofounded and writes for is sold in boutiques nationally. Gaddis currently stars in the TV show she cocreated and produced *Lishy Lou and Lucky Too* as part of the Emmy Award–winning children's series *The Friday Zone* on PBS/PBS KIDS.

Alongside her husband, Lucky Diaz, she is the cofounder and performer for Latin Grammy Award–winning Lucky Diaz and the Family Jam Band. Their children's music has topped the charts at Sirius XM and is *People* magazine's No. 1 album of the year—playing Los Angeles Festival of Books, Target Stage, the Smithsonian, the Getty Museum, Madison Square Park, Legoland, New York City's Symphony Space, and more.

Their song "Falling" has been used in Coca-Cola's national ad campaign.

As a stand-up comic and improviser, Gaddis has headlined the nation at the World Famous Comedy Store, New York Comedy Club—and has been named one of the funniest upcoming female comics by *Entertainment Weekly*. As a performer, Alisha has appeared on Broadway, and at the Sydney Opera House, Second City Hollywood, Improv Olympic West, Upright Citizens Brigade, and the Comedy Central Stage, as well as touring with her acclaimed solo shows *Step-Parenting: The Last Four-Letter Word*, and *The Search for Something Grand*. She has appeared on MTV, CBS, CNN, Univision, NBC, and A&E, and has voiced many national campaigns. Gaddis is a proud SAG/AFTRA, NARAS, LARAS, and AEA member.

She loves her husband the most.

www.alishagaddis.com

JEFF BOGLE abandoned his cushy corporate gig in 2008 for the far more rewarding career of Dad and to attempt to be funny-ish whilst writing and podcasting about fatherhood, travel, and All Things Childhood on his site, Out With The Kids (OWTK). He thinks it's rad that his work frequently appears on the Huffington Post and PBS, among other digital sites and paper rags, but he's still anxiously awaiting his debutant role as Deadbeat Dad in a *Law & Order* episode. He's married to an adorable redheaded gal who's been laughing at his jokes and believing in his ability to pull off one hair-brained idea after the next since the moment they met. Together, they've spawned a pair of hilarious, strange, and lovely young ladies. Jeff considers himself one of the most fortunate guys in the world, although he often needs to be reminded of this fact.

OWTK.com

MERYL BRANCH-McTIERNAN is a comedic novelist, screenwriter, and blogger for the Huffington Post. She has great admiration for those who perform monologues, but was told by her high school acting teachers that she was much better at writing than acting. A native New Yorker, she traveled West in pursuit of her dream of writing for the small screen. She has trained at Second City Hollywood and received a BS at Syracuse University's S.I. Newhouse School of Public Communications. She is still trying to prove that BS wasn't an acronym for bullshit.
www.huffingtonpost.com/meryl-branchmctiernan

STEVE BRIAN   I am an actor, writer, theater artist, and film-maker currently living in Portland, OR. After receiving my MFA from the Theatre School at DePaul in Chicago and calling Los Angeles home over the past three years, I have moved back to Oregon to grow roots, raise a kid, and drink more coffee than my adrenal glands can handle. Above all things, I believe that you need to be comfortable with the words you are speaking during an audition. So feel free to change a few words here and there and know that you have my blessing...but don't go crazy. If you want to get in touch, you can reach me through my website.
www.stevebrian.com

CARLA CACKOWSKI is a person who does things. She toured the world performing comedy (on a boat!) with comedy troupe the Second City, and she currently teaches improvisation to wonderful dreamers at the Second City in Los Angeles. Carla has written and performed five comedic solo shows that have played in superfun places like Los Angeles, New York City, San Diego, and Austin. She's a member of the Solo Collective, a theater company currently in residence at VS. Theater in Los Angeles. Several of her monologues were published in *Women's Comedic*

Monologues That Are Actually Funny (Applause Books, 2014). She is a member of SAG-AFTRA and, as a voice-over artist, has been featured on television shows such as *iCarly*, *Pretty Little Liars*, and *Cougar Town*. Carla was a writer on *Lishy Lou and Lucky Too*, an adorably hilarious children's show that aired on PBS KIDS. Carla really loves her family and friends and hopes that even if she never procreates, two hundred years from now someone will think of her when they read her monologues in this book.

www.carlacackowski.com

TAMMY JO DEAREN is a Los Angeles–based comic and show producer. She has been called a "comedic jackhammer." She entertains the audience with her high-energy, surprising edge and unique perspective. Having the special opportunity of performing weekly at the World Famous Comedy Store on the Sunset Strip, she has performed side by side with Judd Apatow, Bill Burr, Sarah Silverman, Bret Ernst, and more. Tony Joey is Tammy Jo's alter ego, best summed up as a chauvinistic douchebag. Tony's strong East Coast accent, goatee, and slicked-back hair is his signature winning combination. Fist pumps and leg kicks punctuate his social commentary shout-outs and declarations. He is a disgusting pig that speaks louder than his elevated voice. So wrong and so funny…it's Tony Joey!

@tammyjodearen

BRANDON ECON studied *Magic: The Gathering* and theater at the University of Utah in Salt Lake City. He has a cat named Katan, and you may have seen him shouting on stages all across Los Angeles. He is currently writing a trashy novel set in a sugar shack in Quebec, and a comedy horror film about a werewolf who writes other people's biographies. He voiced a Swedish paper bag puppet in a Fandango commercial and recently built a spice rack which he is very proud of. If you dive really deep into Google, you'd be able to see when and where he is performing next—but be warned, he typically pretends to be an alpha male or a Velociraptor so it might not be worth it in the end. He was born in Ohio but doesn't like to talk about that. A werewolf wrote this.

TANNER EFINGER is primarily an improv comedian. He has worked with ComedySportz (NYC), Bruised Fruits (NYC), Proletarian Improv (L.A.), Oxford Imps (UK), and many others. He has taught improv at schools including Phillips Academy Andover, Phillips Exeter Academy, Princeton University, Golden Performing Arts (L.A.), and Charterhouse School (UK). As he types this, he is hungry and wondering if he should have lunch. He has written for many blogs and magazines, has written two screenplays and one stage play, and is now working on his first novel.

HANNAH GANSEN is a Los Angeles–based comedian, writer, and singer-songwriter. She has performed at numerous festivals (Fringe, Women in Comedy, Hollywood, L.A. Comedy), clubs (Laugh Factory, Comedy Central Stage, Comedy Store, the Apollo, Zanie's, the Improv, IO West, IO Chicago, Flappers, Icehouse), and many underground, alternative comedy venues. Her music/comedy album, *Al the Bum*, is available on iTunes and Amazon.

www.hannahgansen.com

JESSICA GLASSBERG is a comedy writer and stand-up co-median. For ten years, she was the head writer on *The Jerry Lewis MDA Telethon* and performed stand-up on the nationally syndicated show five times. She has also written for Disney XD, "A Hollywood Christmas at The Grove" for *Extra*, and the Screen

Actors Guild Awards (where her jokes were highlighted on E!'s *The Soup*, EntertainmentWeekly.com, and Hollywood.com). Additionally, Glassberg was a featured performer on *The History of the Joke with Lewis Black* on the History Channel. Her monologue "Always Awkward" was published in the book *Women's Comedic Monologues That Are Actually Funny* (Applause Books, 2014). She currently produces and hosts a stand-up comedy showcase in Los Angeles called "Laugh, Drink, Repeat." Jessica is also a prolific digital writer, with her work featured on HelloGiggles.com, Reductress.com, Kveller.com, AbsrdCOMEDY.com, and Torquemag.io. For upcoming shows, clips, and writings samples, check out her website. Follow her on Twitter at twitter.com/Glassberg.

www.jessicaglassberg.com

ANDY GOLDENBERG grew up in Florida and graduated from the University of Miami with a BFA in theater, but considers himself a triple-threat Angeleno. With several commercials and TV roles under his belt, his big break came as Adam Sandler's acting double and scene partner in *Jack and Jill* (2011): when Adam played Jack, Andy played Jill. His Goldentusk YouTube channel has more than 50 million views, with *Time Out New York* film critic Keith Uhlich nicknaming him the Theme Song Sondheim. He was a coverboy of the *Nice Jewish Guys Calendar*, wrote and performed sketch comedy with National Lampoon, and recently published a children's book called *Peter, the Paranoid Pumpkin*. He regularly performs with the record-breaking improv team, Freedom Snatch. For the bravest of actors, Andy challenges you to perform his bio for your next audition.

www.youtube.com/goldentusk

DEBORAH GROSS is a playwright/producer/performer based in New York City and Los Angeles. She is a graduate of the Roy

H. Park School of Communications-Ithaca College. Deb studied improv and sketch writing at the Upright Citizens Brigade Theatre in L.A. and New York, and is a graduate of the Los Angeles Second City Conservatory Program. Her sketches have been performed at the L.A. Fest of Sketch, the L.A. Improv Festival, and the San Francisco Sketch Fest. Her blog *Conversations with Deb* won the Other Network Comedy Contest and ran as a stage show at UCB in New York and L.A. Her one-act *The Third Date* was named Best in Fest at the 2013 Hollywood Fringe Festival. She is currently a contributing writer on Someecards.com.

www.conversationswithdeb.com

JP KARLIAK   Voice-over artist, writer, solo performer, and snappy dresser, JP hails from the "Electric City" Scranton, Pennsylvania. His voice has fallen out of the mouths of *Marvel* heroes and villains, a werewolf nemesis of the *Skylanders*, and a college kid buzzed on Red Bull, among others. On screen, he planned a fancy party for Sarah Michelle Gellar and delivered singing telegrams to the *Real Husbands of Hollywood*. A graduate of the USC School of Theatre, iO West, and Second City Training Center, he has written numerous short films and plays produced in locales around the country. His full-length solo show, *Donna/Madonna*, has garnered awards at the United Solo, New York International Fringe, and San Francisco Fringe Festivals. He can always be found at fancy chocolate boutiques or on his website.

jpkarliak.com

MARK HARVEY LEVINE has had over 1,100 productions of his plays all over the world from New York to Bucharest to Jakarta to London. His work has been seen at such theaters as the Actors Theatre of Louisville, City Theatre of Miami, and the Kennedy Center in Washington, DC. Evenings of his short plays have been produced at the Edinburgh Fringe Festival, as well as in Amsterdam, Sao Paulo, Seoul, Sydney, New York, Los Angeles, Boston, Indianapolis, Columbus, Providence, and other cities. An evening of his plays had a National Tour of Brazil from 2007 through 2010. His work has been translated and performed in eight languages. His plays have won numerous awards and been performed at numerous festivals, such as the Alan Minieri Award at New York's 15-Minute Play Festival, and the In A New York Minute one-page play festival (five times in a row!). He currently lives in Pasadena, California, with his lovely wife and son.

www.markharveylevine.com

EITAN LOEWENSTEIN is a writer/actor/director in Los Angeles. Yes, one of those. After graduating from the University of California, Santa Barbara, with a degree in electrical engineering, Eitan decided to forgo the exciting, uncertain world of engineering for a humdrum, predictable career in the entertainment industry. Eitan has written various short films, features, and a web series. Some have been filmed, most have not. Eitan recently won the first ever WGA Mighty Pen Commendation. As an actor Eitan has appeared in a respectable number of commercials and a few TV shows. Eitan has also directed a few short films, some of which are funny. Eitan's most popular piece of writing is ironically a piece on "How to Write a Biography." It is ironic because this biography is pretty "meh."

eitanthewriter.com

KENNY MADRID draws most of his inspiration from a troubled upbringing as a white, upper-middle class, cisgender male. Why is he a writer? Well, if you can find another profession that pays him to make dick jokes all day, he's all ears. Kenny attended San Diego State University before moving to Los Angeles to sell out and get rich. He has hosted a radio show, worked at multiple political offices, an elementary school, a movie studio, and a number of<<OK?>> production companies but simply tells his friends and family that he "makes movies," because anything more specific would confuse them. He can usually be found at his local watering hole on the corner of where "shitty" meets "nice," rolling his eyes at bar patrons who complain that movies aren't good anymore.

LEAH MANN grew up in Washington, DC, and graduated with a degree in theater from Brown University in 2003. Since moving to Los Angeles in 2004, she has written several screenplays, television specs, short stories, and one novel than no one will ever see. Her short story "Going Solo" was published alongside work by prominent authors such as Neil Gaiman and Ray Bradbury in the horror anthology *Psychos: Serial Killers, Depraved Madmen, and the Criminally Insane*. Leah currently works as a production designer, property master, and set decorator. She digs crosswords, hikes, and art projects, reads a lot of fiction, and doesn't own a dog—even though it seems like she ought to.

leahmann.com

KELLY MOLL was most recently published in the hilarious first book of monologues compiled by Alisha Gaddis, *Women's Comedic Monologues That Are Actually Funny* (Applause Books, 2014). By day she is a corporate event planner and is required to wear a suit and respectable heels regularly. By night, she is a writer with visible tattoos and an affinity for swearing and sarcasm. She is currently "nearly finished" with numerous works-in-progress, which range from the biographical to the highly imagined. She does her best thinking while watching the banks of the Mississippi River blaze by on the back of her husband's motorcycle. With a few more trips down the river, she hopes to knock one of the WIP's out of the park and end her tour of duty in the corporate world. She lives in Minneapolis with the aforementioned husband.

GINA NICEWONGER has been "writing in the moment" by performing improv comedy for over ten years. She has written and performed in shows at the Annoyance Theater and Improv Olympic in Chicago and, more recently, at various theaters throughout Los Angeles. Gina wrote one-acts produced by Studio C Artists and enjoys writing sketch comedy with the groups BBQ Committee, Chrissy and Gina, and Hot Lunch. When not making stuff up, Gina enjoys teaching elementary school.

JEFF PASSINO is a Los Angeles–based writer and director. At age four, he won first place in a talent show in his hometown of Perrysburg, OH, by singing *The Greatest American Hero* theme song. After that, Hollywood seemed like the only real place for him. Since his arrival in 1998, Jeff has worked in various aspects of the film and TV industry. He is currently directing a web series he wrote for NBC/Universal. Additionally, Jeff is a photographer, a stand-up comic, and an improviser who has performed on various stages throughout L.A. In his spare time, he bakes pies that friends have described as being "pretty good." He ran the L.A. Marathon twice, though he didn't win either time.

jeffpassino.com

CHRIS QUINTOS is a writer/actor/housewife who is lucky enough to live in both San Francisco and Los Angeles. She loves being right, hanging out with her dog, Beta, shopping in bulk, and books. She dislikes scary movies, walking on sidewalk grates, cleaning her car, and clowns. She'd like to thank her husband for being wonderful and handsome (AND VERY PATIENT). Many thanks to her family and friends who let her be 1,000 percent Chris, whatever that means. Thanks also to Alisha Gaddis for being a kick-ass lady. Chris cannot believe she is being published in a book—an actual book! Follow, stalk, chat @chrisquintos.

www.chrisquintos.com

RACHEL RAINES grew up in St. Louis, where she spent time working in the performing arts and volunteering in theater. She attended the American Musical and Dramatic Academy in California, studying film and stage acting as well as being trained in improvisational comedy. She has worked as a freelance writer for seven years, and her past work includes an essay in *The Diamond Project: Ordinary Women Leading Extraordinary Lives*, edited by Cynthia Hurst, and various articles for online social media. She currently lives in Los Angeles.

ALESSANDRA RIZZOTTI has written for *GOOD*, *Heeb*, *Smith*, *Hello Giggles*, and The Neave. She's also been published in three Harper Perennial books with her six word memoirs, and is now working on a novel about finding her father. She currently edits for *Backstage Magazine*, bridging the gap between filmmakers and actors.

alessandrarizzotti.com

KATE RUPPERT My drink is vodka. I don't go on dates. I'm funny. I have to write things down. Small talk is annoying. I'm left-handed. I cannot spell. I love red meat. I'm decisive. I hate the phone. I don't keep food in my house. I'm ambidextrous. I can't sleep on airplanes or in a car. Dogs, children, parents, and black people love me. I love to tip. I am unapologetically in love with TV. I think spontaneity is overrated. I'm never passive-aggressive. My cell phone is always charging. I'm efficient mostly so I can be lazy. I have ChapStick, a nail file, a hair clip, and Post-its within arm's reach at all times. I don't dance. Ever. I prefer to watch than participate. I'd rather stay home every time. I'm awkward and clumsy. I have very little pride. I tend to speak in hyperbole. I don't check my messages. Food is my most favorite thing. I love to sleep. I'm acutely aware. I watch *General Hospital*.

CHRISSY SWINKO is a writer and performer in Los Angeles. She has written for and performed on several notable stages including the Comedy Central Stage, iO West, iO Chicago, the Second City Hollywood, and Comedy Sportz Chicago. She has studied writing and improv comedy at UCB, and with the Groundlings, the Second City, and the iO Theater. She grew up in Ohio and is a graduate of Denison University. Her hobbies include eating chocolate, reading, and watching movies. As the founder of Women Made It, she loves to help other people tell their stories and achieve their creative goals. Find her online at @omg4reals and www.ChrissySwinko.com. She thanks you for reading and performing her monologue. Have fun out there and "break a leg!"

chrissyswinko.com

MATT TAYLOR hails from a pestilent wasteland just short of the Scottish border with England. Neither the English or Scottish people wanted anything to do with him or his foul-smelling city, so he fled to the United States after telling a series of outrageous lies to an infinitely more attractive American woman so she would marry him. Before he started trying to be funny for a living, he served in the Royal Marines Commandos for a decade, and saw action in both Iraq and Afghanistan. He is renowned for being the only soldier in coalition history that found Baghdad much more pleasant than his own hometown. He now resides in the much more agreeable Pasadena, California, with his perpetually misled wife. He is not trusted with children or pets after he once put his spouse's goldfish "back in its cage" before retiring to bed.

http://newsfury.blogspot.com

LYNN TRICKEY is an actor, writer, and improviser originally from Seattle. She's studied Meisner Technique at the Elizabeth Mestnik Acting Studio, improv comedy at UCB, the Groundlings, and iO West, and has a BA in theater from Pitzer College. She's written and performed sketch comedy at Second City Hollywood, at iO West Sketch Festival, in Character workshops, and at the Comedy Central Stage. Lynn performs weekly in and around Los Angeles with the improv teams Wheelhouse, Big Bennessy, and Doctor Who Live.

www.lynntrickey.com

KATHY YAMAMOTO is a Los Angeles native, although she wishes she had been born in Warsaw, Poland. She could've been born in Poland, but her dad made her mom immigrate before her birth so she might one day be president. From an early age, she realized she had a knack for making others laugh, even earning the title of "Funniest Girl in Traditional Japanese Dance Class," an honor admittedly earned without much competition. Now, instead of governing the free world, Kathy spends her time writing and performing comedy. In addition to performing improv and stand-up around town, Kathy is a writer on iO West's topical sketch team, Top Story Weekly. You can find her on YouTube in her web series, *Kat&Nat*, and on Twitter @yamaDRAMA.

Acknowledgments

A lot of people are awesome. Some people are more awesome in regards to this book. They get extra thanks from Alisha Gaddis:

Thank you to Sara Camilli—best literary agent ever. I adore you. You are like family to me now. And look—now we have a series! This is just the beginning.

Thank you to all the writers. You all put yourselves out there. It is hard to be funny, and extra super hard to be funny on paper in a particular format. You guys did it and it is amazing!

Thank you to Applause Theatre & Cinema Books (especially John Cerullo and Marybeth Keating). You guys have given me so much guidance, support, and freedom. I couldn't ask for more in a publisher. And thank you to copyeditor Patty Hammond. You make all our funny writing grammatically correct, readable, and even more hilarious!

Thank you to my parents, family, and friends. Obviously. You all are the best.

And the super biggest thanks of all to my handsome husband. You are my ideal match. Thank you for inspiring me to live past my largest, most grand dream. You make me better every single day. I cannot thank you enough. But I will keep trying.

Other Monologue and Scene Books

Best Contemporary Monologues for Kids Ages 7-15
edited by Lawrence Harbison
9781495011771 ....$16.99

Best Contemporary Monologues for Men 18-35
edited by Lawrence Harbison
9781480369610 ....$16.99

Best Contemporary Monologues for Women 18-35
edited by Lawrence Harbison
9781480369627 ....$16.99

Best Monologues from The Best American Short Plays, Volume Three
edited by William W. Demastes
9781480397408 ....$19.99

Best Monologues from The Best American Short Plays, Volume Two
edited by William W. Demastes
9781480385481 ....$19.99

Best Monologues from The Best American Short Plays, Volume One
edited by William W. Demastes
9781480331556 ....$19.99

Childsplay
A Collection of Scenes and Monologues for Children
edited by Kerry Muir
9780879101886 ....$16.99

Duo!
The Best Scenes for Two for the 21st Century
edited by Joyce E. Henry, Rebecca Dunn Jaroff, and Bob Shuman
9781557837028 ....$19.99

Duo!
Best Scenes for the 90's
edited by John Horvath, Lavonne Mueller, and Jack Temchin
9781557830302 ....$18.99

In Performance
Contemporary Monologues for Men and Women Late Teens to Twenties
by JV Mercanti
9781480331570 ....$18.99

In Performance
Contemporary Monologues for Men and Women Late Twenties to Thirties
by JV Mercanti
9781480367470 ....$16.99

The Monologue Audition
A Practical Guide for Actors
by Karen Kohlhaas
9780879102913 ....$22.99

One on One
The Best Men's Monologues for the 21st Century
edited by Joyce E. Henry, Rebecca Dunn Jaroff, and Bob Shuman
9781557837011 ....$18.99

One on One
The Best Women's Monologues for the 21st Century
edited by Joyce E. Henry, Rebecca Dunn Jaroff, and Bob Shuman
9781557837004 ....$18.99

One on One: Playing with a Purpose
Monologues for Kids Ages 7-15
edited by Stephen Fife and Bob Shuman with contributing editors Eloise Rollins-Fife and Marit Shuman
9781557838414 ....$16.99

One on One: The Best Monologues for Mature Actors
edited by Stephen Fife
9781480360198 ....$19.99

Scenes and Monologues of Spiritual Experience from the Best Contemporary Plays
edited by Roger Ellis
9731480331563 ....$19.99

Scenes and Monologues from Steinberg/ATCA New Play Award Finalists, 2008–2012
edited by Bruce Burgun
9781476868783 ....$19.99

Soliloquy!
The Shakespeare Monologues
edited by Michael Earley and Philippa Keil
9780936839783 Men's Edition ...$11.95
9780936839790 Women's Edition ...$14.95

Teen Boys' Comedic Monologues That Are Actually Funny
edited by Alisha Gaddis
9781480396791 ....$14.99

Women's Comedic Monologues That Are Actually Funny
edited by Alisha Gaddis
9781480360426................$14.99

APPLAUSE
THEATRE & CINEMA BOOKS

AN IMPRINT OF
HAL•LEONARD

Prices, contents, and availability subject to change without notice.

0515